Liberation Theology

LIBERATION THEOLOGY
From Dialogue to Confrontation

Leonardo Boff
Clodovis Boff

Translated by Robert R. Barr

1817

Harper & Row, Publishers, San Francisco

Cambridge, Hagerstown, New York, Philadelphia, Washington
London, Mexico City, São Paulo, Singapore, Sydney

Parts I and II of this book were originally published in Portuguese as *Teologia da Libertação no Debate Atual* in 1985 by Editora Vozes Limitada, Petrópolis, Brazil.
The English translation for this edition is by Robert R. Barr.

FIRST EDITION

Library of Congress Cataloging-in-Publication Data

Boff, Leonardo.
  Liberation theology.

  "Parts I and II of this book were originally
published in Portuguese as Teologia de libertação no
debate atual in 1985 . . ."—T.p. verso.
  1. Liberation theology. I. Boff, Clodovis.
II. Boff, Leonardo. Teologia de libertação no debate
atual. III. Title
BT83.57.B597 1986   261.8   85-51997
ISBN 0-86683-528-8

86 87 88 89 90 MPC 10 9 8 7 6 5 4 3 2 1

CONTENTS

INTRODUCTION

They are hungry, they are poor, they are exploited, and they die young. This is the reality confronting the theology of liberation. This leaves no one indifferent, of course, and this is why liberation theology stirs up so much debate, rejection, criticism, and enthusiasm.

In the maelstrom of positions taken vis-à-vis this terrible reality, we must never lose sight of the basic problem. We must always maintain sufficient serenity to keep our emotions from clouding our vision. The materials presented here are intended as a contribution to the current debate on the theology of liberation—this chant of the Third World transformed into a reflection of messianic hope for a society of freedom, a society that will become a communion of brothers and sisters. May these chapters generate light for the path and warmth for the journey.

I

Liberation Theology

1

A PUBLIC PHENOMENON

With the arrival of the theology of liberation on the contemporary scene, theology is no longer for theologians alone. Now it involves whole people of God, clergy and laity alike. Theology has become genuinely and truly *ecclesial*.

More than this, liberation theology has overflowed the very borders of the Church and become a *public* phenomenon. We hear it discussed, and heatedly discussed, in the media, in the halls of academe, in union meetings, in political gatherings—even in cafés and restaurants. One would think the time of the Council of Nicaea had returned (A.D. 325). Then the question of the day was Arianism—whether Christ was truly and fully God—and the excitement of the question overflowed the halls of scholarship and swept into the streets, as Saint Gregory of Nyssa recounts.

All over town you hear all about it, in the market, the forum, and the streets—from the clothing merchant, the money-changer, and the businessman. You ask for the exchange rate and you get a disquisition on "begotten and unbegotten." The price of bread? The answer comes, "The Father is greater than the Son—and subject to him!" You ask if the baths are open, and in response you hear that the Son was created from nothing.

What is this malaise, this frenzied excitement, this mind-altering affliction? [Migne, *Patrologia Graeca*, vol. 46, col. 557]

More than a millenium and a half after Saint Gregory's

time, the phenomenon has returned. Why all the excitement about theology?

Because the theology of liberation is *more than just a theology*. It represents the Church of a whole continent—a Church caught up in the historical process of a people on the move. There are *people* behind liberation theology, there is struggle, there is life. The theology of liberation is symptomatic of a *process*, a process at once ecclesial and social. Behind liberation theology stand not books, but people. What is at stake is that "telltale difference" between theory and practice. $B \neq B$

It is its *pre-theological background*, then, that stirs such broad interest in liberation theology today. The general importance of this new theology—not just its importance for Latin America—has been recognized by some of today's most representative theologians. Edward Schillebeeckx, for instance, was asked in an interview, "Who are the best theologians today?" And his answer was, "The most competent theologians of the West today, including both Europe and the Americas, are the liberation theologians. We learn a great deal from them. We're too academic. The liberation theologians make us reflect out of the life of the Christian community" (*Il Regno Attualità*, no. 18 [October 15, 1984], pp. 446–47). Karl Rahner, on more than one occasion, and Hans Urs von Balthasar on the occasion of his recent Paul VI Prize, in June 1984, have pointed to the theology of liberation as the newest and most vital phenomenon on the theological landscape.

This theological vitality is nourished by the vitality of the Church and vice versa. Spanish theologian Juan Alfaro, who teaches at the Gregorian University in Rome, put it this way:

Latin America today . . . is the scene of a most important occurrence for the entire Church—not only for the Latin American church, but for the *whole* Church. . . . What is new today is the appearance in Latin America of a new Christian awareness of what it is to be genuinely Christian, a new awareness of a world of brotherhood and justice. In my view this represents a most important change of direction, one which will have repercussions—and is already having repercussions—in Europe. . . . This contribution of liberation theology is far and away theology's best: to stir Christian faith to the responsibility to make a Christian commitment to justice. This shift in direction is its highest merit. . . . My concern is not so much that liberation theology is under attack, but that this new Christianity, just born is being destroyed. . . . This is [Christian] responsibility, not to trample on this new Christian seed that is sending up its first shoots. [*Il Regno Attualità*, no. 14 (July 15, 1984), pp. 323–24]

The renowned German theologian Johannes B. Metz has expressed the same thought:

The Latin American churches are showing us a transformation process of unheard-of proportions—one which, in my view, is endowed with a providential importance for the whole Church, and in which, in one manner or another, we are all involved. [*Al di là della religione borghese* (Brescia: Queriniana, 1981), p. 18]

This broader, world-wide relevance of the theology of liberation makes it understandable why the Holy See would wish to take a position on the matter, as it has in its recent *Instruction on Certain Aspects of the "Theology of Liberation."* In doing so, it has reopened the question and awakened new interest on the part of Christians.

On another level—in the extra-ecclesial area—we know that the centers of world power are watching the Latin American church process, and watching its theology, very closely. The reason, of course, is simply the social and political implications of this ecclesial process. We need

only consider the Rockefeller and the Rand Corporation
reports of the late 1970s. More recently, the famous "Santa
Fe Document," of May 1980, published by the Committee
of Santa Fe for the Council for Inter-American Security,
declares that "American foreign policy should begin to
mount a counterattack on (and not merely react against)
liberation theology." It considers this theology to be a
"political weapon" of "Marxist-Leninist forces" for the
purpose of "infiltrating the religious community" and
spreading ideas "against private ownership and produc-
tive capitalism" (part 2, par. 3).

Nor is there any dearth of studies sponsored by the op-
posite power center, in the Soviet Union, on the phenomenon of the Latin American Church and its new theology.

But much more significant than any attention paid to
the theology of liberation at the pinnacles of power is the
involvement of the common people, the "grassroots," with
this theology. Ultimately the reason for this involvement is
that liberation theology *speaks of the concrete life of the people,* especially through its interpretation of today's mighty
longing for liberation among them. It is perhaps the greatest merit of the theology of liberation to have succeeded in
doing with theology what Socrates did with philosophy.
As Cicero tells us, Socrates "brought philosophy down
from the clouds to earth." In other words, he made it walk
on its own feet.

2

THE EXPERIENCE OF A LIBERATING FAITH

Before the emergence of a theology of liberation at the close of the 1960s, a full-fledged liberation praxis was already under way in Latin America. Before liberation theology there were the prophetic bishop, the committed lay person, and liberation communities. A life *practice* was well under way even in the early 1960s. The *theology* of liberation, then, came in a "second moment." It came as the *expression* of this liberation praxis on the part of the Church. Liberation theology is the *theology of a liberation Church*—a Church with a preferential option for solidarity with the poor.

Of course, the theology of liberation is not the mere *reflex* of a liberation faith. It is also a *reflection* on that faith—an in-depth explanation, a purification, a systematization of that faith. In other words: liberation theology enlightens and stimulates the life and practice of the actual, concrete Church.

To be sure, a *reciprocal relation* obtains between action and reflection—faith action and theological reflection in the Church maintain a two-way relationship. Still, theology is more an effect than a cause of the practice of faith, and it is a cause only because it is an effect.

Removed from its *Sitz im Leben*, withdrawn from the vital context of its origin and development, the theology of liberation becomes altogether incomprehensible. Liberation theology cannot be understood merely by reading books and articles. The books and articles absolutely must be connected with the soil of the Church and of society, from which these writings have sprung, inasmuch as they seek to interpret and illuminate that Church and that society.

It is *only within a process*, then, a fabric whose warp and woof are suffering and hope, that liberation theology is born, and therefore understood. From above, or from without, there is no understanding it at all. We might even go so far as to say that the theology of liberation can be understood only by two groupings of persons: the poor, and those who struggle for justice at their side—only by those who hunger for bread, and by those who hunger for justice in solidarity with those hungering for bread. Conversely, liberation theology is not understood, nor can it be understood, by the satiated and satisfied—by those comfortable with the status quo.

The implication here is that, down at the "base," antecedent to all theologizing, is an option for life, a particular, determinate faith experience, the taking of a position vis-à-vis the concrete world in which we live. It is from a pretheological element as one's starting point, then, that one is totally "for," or totally "against," the theology of liberation.

In other words, it is crucial to grasp liberation theology in its locus. Theologians of liberation must be read not in the ivory towers of certain departments of theology (to borrow an image from Pope John Paul II), but in the slums, in the miserable neighborhoods of the destitute, in the factories, on the plantations—wherever an oppressed people live, suffer, struggle, and die.

To pretend to "discuss liberation theology" *without seeing the poor* is to miss the whole point, for one fails to see the central problem of the theology being discussed. For the kernel and core of liberation theology is not theology but liberation. It is not the theologian but the poor who count in this theology. Were the theology of liberation somehow to pass into oblivion, would the problem it has raised thereby be solved? To fail to see this is to fit the Brazilian proverb to a tee: "You heard the rooster crow, but you don't know where."

We must face the fact. For many persons, a living, direct experience of poverty and of the people's struggle with poverty will be required of them before they will be able to understand this theology. Cardinal Daneels, Archbishop of Brussels, on his return from a visit to Brazil, grasped this very clearly:

There is something tragic in what is going on in and around the theology of liberation today. Liberation theology begins with a very acute, very profound sensitivity to poverty. We see this poverty every day on television. It is another matter, however, to see it on the spot—to allow it to penetrate all five senses, to let ourselves be touched by the suffering of the poor, to feel their anguish, to experience the filth of the slums sticking to our skin. . . . This is problem number one: the plight of the poor. . . . We cannot let these people down! We must support their theologians. [*Entraide et fraternité* newswire, September 20, 1984]

The *Instruction* of the Congregation for the Doctrine of the Faith, then, *does not impugn the theology of liberation at its root*. It shows extreme severity with regard to its current performance. (Cardinal Daneels, a member of the Congregation, describes the target of the document's criticism as "a caricature, a bad liberation theology," which "does not exist in this form" [ibid.]). Far from pulling the theoretical rug from under the theology of liberation, the *Instruction* only provides that theology with a *new and vigorous endorsement*. The document actually bestows its seal of approval on the actual basis of liberation theology. So long as the spring remains unclogged, the river may meander, or even be dammed up, but it will never run dry. This must be said to the *Instruction's* credit, whatever dust it may have raised to cloud the issue. After all, this is *the* question, *the* interest, *the* issue of the *Instruction* and liberation theology alike: the actual liberation of the poor, and not the theology of this liberation.

We must also cite another great merit of the Roman document. It has consecrated and guaranteed the possibility and the legitimacy of an actual theology of liberation. This used to be hotly contested by certain strident elements in the Church. Of course, the question of how this legitimate theological project is to be implemented is another matter, and herein lies the *Instruction's* great shortcoming. But at all events, it must be granted that, whatever may have to be said of the basis of the Vatican animadversions, liberation theology is on the right track. It may have its limits as we have it today—its limits, its ambiguities, yes, and even its errors. It recognizes this. But its course is true, and this is what is crucial. It is the same with any organized reflection.

A FAITH REFLECTION ON
THE PRAXIS OF LIBERATION

The theology of liberation is the thinking of the faith under the formality of a leaven of historical transformation—as the "salt of the earth" and the "light of the world," as the theological virtue of charity exercised in the area of the social.

More simply, the theology of liberation is reflection on the life of the Christian community from a standpoint of its contribution to liberation. "Life" here is a richer and more flexible concept than that of "praxis," which is an external activity of historical transformation. We might be tempted to represent the theology of liberation as a kind of "chemical reaction":

Faith + Oppression → Liberation Theology

The social or political dimension of faith is the new aspect (not the only aspect) of the faith that is emphasized by the theology of liberation. We explore a specific "integral" or "constitutive part" of the "evangelization or mission" of the Church: "action on behalf of justice, and participation in the transformation of the world" (1971 Synod document, "Justice in the World," no. 6, in *Acta Apostolicae Sedis*, 63:924).

The theology of liberation seeks to demonstrate that the kingdom of God is to be established not only in the *soul*—

this is the individual personal dimension of the kingdom—and not only in *heaven*—this is its transhistorical dimension—but in relationships among human beings, as well. In other words, the kingdom of God is to be established in social projects, and this is its historical dimension. In sum, liberation theology is a theology that seeks to take history, and Christians' historical responsibility, seriously.

Christians today are faced with an enormous, unprecedented challenge. Today, as we read in the documents of Vatican II, the Church faces a "new age in human history" (*Gaudium et Spes*, no. 54). Medellín translates this novelty as follows, where Latin America is concerned:

> We stand on the threshold of a new age in the history of our continent—an age bursting with a desire for total emancipation, for liberation from all manner of servitude. . . . [Medellín Final Document, Introduction to the Conclusion, no. 4]

For perhaps the first time in history, the faith of the Christian community faces this challenge: to make a determined contribution—and may it be decisive!—to the building of a new society, in which the great "social dominations" will be no more.

In the first Christian centuries, the faith discharged a function, generally speaking, of *protest against the social order*. Then, during the long Constantinian era, the faith developed a function, predominantly, of the *conservation of the status quo*. Today the moment in history has arrived for the faith to perform a function of *social construction*. The end and aim of the theology of liberation is to serve as an echo of and a response to this immense challenge facing the Church, especially since the time of *Rerum Novarum*.

A NEW METHOD
OF DOING THEOLOGY

The novelty of liberation theology does not lie only in the historical challenge of which we have just spoken. The modern social teaching of the Church, European "political theology," and, still more directly, the theology of the "signs of the times" as practiced in *Gaudium et Spes* have all anticipated it here. All have been an attempt to meet this same challenge.

The novelty of the theology of liberation also, and especially, resides in its manner of developing this modern thematic. The key to the new approach is the praxis of liberation. In the theology of liberation we have a bond—intimate but not rigid—between theory and practice, between theology and the life of faith.

The method practiced by the theology of liberation, we observe, is neither exclusively inductive nor exclusively deductive. It is both of these at once: it is *dialectical*. It is simply a matter of the "mutual challenge" of Gospel and life (*Evangelli Nuntiandi*, no. 29). Only thus, as it happens, may we hope to overcome one of the "more serious errors of our age"—that of a "split" between faith and life, as Vatican II expressed it (*Gaudium et Spes*, no. 43).

This relationship between theory and practice obtains even in the case of the theologian personally. The theologian's link with the community's faith praxis must be concrete and not merely theoretical. Thus inserted into the community of faith, hope, and charity, theologians can practice a theology from within, not one "by extraction."

Affinities between Liberation Theology and Patristic Theology and Biblical Revelation

It is important to note that this dialectic of theory-and-praxis is in no wise originally and exclusively Marxian, even though Marx gave it a specific formulation. This same dialectic lies at the basis both of patristic theology and of biblical revelation itself.

This dialectic of theory and praxis defined the first great Christian theology—that of the Fathers of the early Church. Theologians in the early Christian centuries were simultaneously teachers and pastors. The theology of the Fathers was intimately bound up with the concrete problematic of their lives—theirs and that of their churches. Liberation theology is not as novel as might appear at first blush.

Again, a dialectical relationship between theory and praxis is even at the basis of biblical revelation. The conciliar Constitution on Divine Revelation declares that God revealed himself "in deeds and words intimately interconnected, in such wise that works [our 'praxis'] manifest and corroborate doctrine [theory], and the latter proclaims and elucidates the former" (*Dei Verbum*, no. 2).

The Inalienable Dimensions of Liberation Theology

Would the theology of liberation then be an integral theology in its own right, or only a particular development, however capital, of theology in general? This question is not as yet very well defined. It is basic, however, and calls for further reflection.

At all events, one thing remains clear. While its theoretical basis may indeed need further development, liberation theology's conviction is firm: faith at once *includes* and *transcends* the demand for social liberation (or the social dimension of liberation).

There can be no doubt about it: liberation theology today primarily develops the social dimension of faith. Hence its name. This is due to the fact that this dimension presents itself, first, as being of the greatest urgency, and second, as the aspect of faith most neglected by past theologians.

By all means, the transcendent dimension of faith (liberation from sin and communion with the Father by grace), so well developed by classical theology, is enthusiastically and unhesitatingly accepted by the theology of liberation. Indeed, it is in virtue of this transcendent dimension that a liberation *theology* is possible at all. Is it not in the light and the vigor of faith in the Father, the risen Lord Jesus, and the Spirit of life, that the theology of liberation speaks of a history of oppression and liberation? In a word, in liberation theology the transcendent dimension of faith is *accepted* in faith, *presupposed* as thematized (or actually thematized), and then *recast* from a point of departure in liberation theology's proper "cultural sensitivity." The basis and point of departure of the theology of liberation is the theological virtue of faith.

Thus it is that the theology of liberation joins its own voice to a symphonic, pluralistic theology—not, however, without issuing a strong challenge to other theological currents, especially where attention to a historical praxis in each concrete situation seems to be neglected.

Two Key Characteristics
of the Theology of Liberation

From what we have observed, the following points are clear. First, the theology of liberation is a profoundly *ecclesial* theology, worked out in intimate, concrete communion with the Christian community, its pastors and its faithful alike. Liberation theology emerges as a service of expression and explanation of the faith, hope, and charity of the community of Christians. Second, the theology of liberation is an altogether *concrete* theology. Its intent is to "think the life problems of the people of God" in order to resolve these problems with the leaven of the Gospel. We have a historical, contextual theology here.

5

MYTHOLOGY OF THE
THEOLOGY OF LIBERATION

Having in the foregoing sketch identified what
the theology of liberation really is, we are now in a position to criticize the myth or caricature that circulates in
its regard.

Myth No. 1: Liberation Theology
Has "Fathers," or "Founders"

When you see a child you have never seen before,
especially if he or she seems to you to be a bit of a "hell-
raiser," you wonder who the parents are. You would like to
unload on them at least some of the responsibility for their
offspring's antics. In the case of liberation theology, there
are some who want to know whom to "blame" for this new
theology's questions. And so we hear of the "fathers of
liberation theology."

We likewise hear of its "founders"—as if the theology of
liberation were a "doctrine" created by the decision of
certain strange minds. And names and dates are listed.
Some critics lift their eyes to the horizons of history and
hark back to a "family tree." The "ancestors" of the theology of liberation would be, we hear, Marx and Bultmann.

In point of fact, as we have seen, this theology is simply

the language of a particular, concrete Church involved with the poor and committed to their liberation. Their faith experience—this new kind of Christianity—can have its developers, its interpreters, surely. These are the representatives, in the realm of theory, of this type of Church, somewhat as the Evangelists are looked on today as the "redactors" of the memory and living faith of the primitive Christian community. But by no means will these persons be the inventors of a new doctrine, which is thereupon "applied" by pastoral ministers and behold, the base Church communities, a popular ministry, prophetic bishops, involved religion, and so on, spring into being!

Further: the theology of liberation is not a "cultural fact." It is, however, the cultural expression of a living process.

In a nutshell, then: the real fathers and mothers of the theology of liberation are the hierarchical Church, in the context of an oppressed, Christian, Latin American people.

Myth No. 2: Liberation Theology Is "Reductionistic"

It is likewise bruited about that the theology of liberation is an entirely "secularized" theology—that it reduces faith to a strictly earthly ideology, hope to a purely temporal eschatology, and love to nothing but a political practice.

Here we are dealing with a precipitant, simplistic—and terrified—interpretation. Surely no interpretative code but an ignorant, ill-willed, or terror-stricken one could read "political too" as "political only," "earth too" as "earth only," or "also, and especially, the poor" as "only the poor," and so on.

It would be an interesting experiment to respond to the

But where does L.T. spend most of its time – EARTHLY CONCER

allegation of reductionism with the classic *riposte:* What about the reductionisms of classical theology, especially in a later, essentialistic scholasticism, that great, vaunted "total theology"? What about *its* reduction of major biblical themes, such as physical poverty, physical liberation in history, social transformation, justice for the laborer, and the like, to "spiritual" poverty, liberation, righteousness, and so on?

We must say it again: The theology of liberation is, and seeks only to be, a discourse permeated with the light of faith, even though this faith may not always be found in thematized form (and still less "cut and dried" in virtue of being thematized).

Admittedly, the basic relationship that the theology of liberation seeks to express, the relationship between salvation and liberation, is not always worded in a perfectly satisfactory manner. But it is essential to grasp the intentionality of its discourse—that is, what it is trying to say, rather than merely what it actually says.

Furthermore and finally: When this imputation of "reductionism" is subjected to verification in the living practice of the theology of liberation in the communities—of which, after all, this theology seeks to be the reflex and reflection—there can no longer be any doubt. One need only watch the people reading the Bible and praying their faith to realize that this allegation is pure myth. Never in the history of Latin America has there been as much praying as in today's basic church communities.

Admittedly, this also means that we in Latin America are better at practice than at theory. But after all, does life not "say" more than discourse does? On our continent transcendence is practice, not rhetoric.

perhaps in an immediate, existential way, but what beyond that?

Myth No. 3: Liberation Theology Is "of Marxist Inspiration"

Liberation theology, so the story goes, is "based" on or "inspired" by Marxism. Certain publications like to dress up their articles on liberation theology with drawings of Karl Marx, guerrillas, rallies, and so on. The theology of liberation likewise "promotes class struggles," we hear, and proclaims that violence is a legitimate means to the all-justifying end of liberation.

This myth is not easy to dispel. Like all myths, it is more emotional than rational. But we must make the attempt. Let us state, once and for all, frankly and unambiguously: by no means is Marxism the moving force, basis, or inspiration of the theology of liberation. Christian faith is. It is the Gospel that is the determining qualifier of the theology of liberation, as it must be of any theology. The Gospel is the heart. All else is adventitious.

Marxism is a secondary, peripheral issue. When Marxism is used at all, it is used only *partially* and *instrumentally*. The popes themselves, the bishops, and many non-Marxist social scientists do the same thing. It is the faith that assimilates or subsumes elements of Marxism, then, and not the other way about. And the assimilation is effected from a point of departure in the community of the poor, so that the elements assimilated are profoundly transformed in the very assimilation, in such a way that the result is no longer Marxism but simply a critical understanding of reality.

We confess: The difficult subsumption of Marxist elements has not always been effected with adequate lucidity, perspicacity, and maturity. But we are improving along the way—serenely, with evangelical caution, but without any fear of the "heresy hunters."

Myth No. 4: Liberation Theology Is an "Unscientific Theology"

We sometimes hear it said that liberation theology is merely pastoral and pragmatic, and thus devoid of the scientific "substance" of North Atlantic theology. Here one really has to wonder whether *scientific* may be confused with *academic*, to the exclusion of the *critical*. The theology of liberation, of course, comes on the scene as a critical theology. As a new theology, it still has a "long way to go." How could it be otherwise? Our new theology must still flesh out a new synthesis of the faith, from its starting point in a new experience of that faith. This is one of its concrete tasks, and it is well aware of this. The *systematicity* of the theology of liberation is yet wanting. But the *method* has been discovered and is being developed.

Let us note, however, that the most important thing for liberation theology is not its scientificity but precisely its *service*. Really, one must ask to what extent so-called "scientific theology" effectively communicates the Gospel, how much ecclesial life it generates. After all, it is not enough to be brilliant; one must also be true. It is not enough to generate books and not generate life.

6

AXES OR PIVOTS OF THE THEOLOGY OF LIBERATION

The grand inspiration of liberation theology's specific endeavor is the *correct "partial" identification of social liberation with salvation, and the correct subordination of the former to the latter—the correct interrelationship between praxis and faith.* The theology of liberation tries to bridge the gap between the Mystery of God and the history of human beings. After all, it is not enough to know the truth of faith: One must also develop the human, historical significance and import of this faith.

The basic question for the theology of liberation is this: What is God for a continent of the poor such as Latin America? How does God reveal himself to the oppressed? What does it mean to be a Christian in a world of the starving?

Once again: It is a ludicrous over-simplification, a facile, indeed calumnious, distortion, to label liberation theology as "horizontalism," or a "politicization of the faith." The theology of liberation seeks only to break away from both extremes—a *spiritualism* oblivious to the world, and a *materialism* oblivious to the Mystery. The theology of liberation has the single-minded aim of joining the spiritual and the material in one—as they are found in human beings, and in the Christian God in Jesus Christ. It seeks to maintain the unity of the history of God with, and within, its vehicle, the history of men and women, in the spirit of Chalcedon: "without confusion, yet without separation."

To put it baldly: Liberation theology is a theology that refuses to resign itself to the use of the Gospel as an alienating or alienated (omitted) ideology. And it is a theology seeking to be the "salt of faith in the soup of life." Of course, the salt comes from a bottomless shaker, so there will always be some salt "in reserve"—salvation includes liberation, yes, but always transcends it.

Now, what is liberation theology in terms of a unitary dialectic? What are its central themes?

None other than theology's classic themes. Only, now they are *articulated upon history by way of projection.* Hence the distinct *accents* of this theology, against a backdrop of revelation in its entirety. With each great theological theme, the theology of liberation inquires: What does this mean for our reality today? What is the meaning and significance of this theme, or this truth, for the oppressed of our continent?

Here is how the theology of liberation articulates certain basic theological themes.

God

a. Liberation theology recovers the image of *God as creator of life,* a God whose glory is the "human being alive." Among a people for whom death is not a simple figure of speech but a daily reality thrust upon their attention in infant mortality, violent conflict, kidnappings, and torture, a theology of God as creator and sustainer of life acquires a piercing relevancy.

b. To an oppressed people, God also appears as *Yahweh the Liberator,* who wills that his people go *free* from all slavery. Here the Exodus is no longer a "typological luxury, serving as counterpoint for a moral-and-spiritual salvation" (José M. González Ruiz), but is the model, in the full sense of the term, of any and every liberation process that has ever been or ever will be—without ceasing to be a "type" of the Paschal mystery, from the viewpoint of salvation-in-its-transcendency.

Christ

In the figure of Jesus, whom it acknowledges as Lord and Son of God, liberation theology accentuates the following traits.

a. His Incarnation is taken "to the hilt." The Word of God assumed not just "human nature" in general, nor even just any random concrete human nature, but the human nature of a particular human being in an altogether determinate *social condition:* that of a poor person, a laborer, who preferred the poor, surrounded himself with them, and identified with them. All of this is seen to be of the utmost significance for a people sunk in the direst imaginable poverty. It is the boast of the poor, not the rich, that Jesus belonged to their social and economic class.

b. Jesus preached the kingdom of God as *absolute, integral liberation*—spiritual, yes, but material as well (liberation from hunger, grief, contempt, and so on), within history and beyond history.

c. Jesus is the historical *victim of a plot laid by the mighty* of his time. This acknowledgment in no way militates against the salvific meaning of his death. On the contrary, it lends this meaning *concrete support:* it was by *this* route, death on a cross, that the Son of God revealed and realized the salvation of human beings.

Mary

Dogmatic mariology (Mary as mother of God, virgin, immaculate, and assumed) is unfailingly maintained by liberation theology, in the "larger picture." But against the background of this larger picture it prefers to stress a *historical* mariology, one more germane to the concrete reality of Latin America.

a. Mary, then, steps forward as *Mary of Nazareth,* a woman who was poor, who toiled with her hands, who was harrassed and persecuted, who was exiled, but who never lost her awareness and her courage (see *Marialis Cultus,* no. 37).

b. Mary is likewise seen as the *woman of the Magnificat*—the prophetic woman of liberation, who had the clear vision and dogged determination to denounce the contrast between the rich and the starving, the mighty and the lowly, and who proclaimed "God's revolution"—God as "avenger of the oppressed" (ibid.).

c. Finally, Mary is the *Mary of popular religion,* the Mary of the Latin American people, this "Marian people." Thus she is seen and experienced as a "protagonist of history," as for example in the struggle for Mexican national liberation, when Father Hidalgo and the liberator Zapata led their people into the struggle

under the banner of the *Morenita,* the "Brown Ma-
donna." As we see, then, Mary is the *woman of the
Incarnation* of the Word of God in history.

These are but a sampling of the Marian accents of the
theology of liberation, but they afford us a glimpse of the
exceedingly rich vein of theological thinking which, to be
sure, calls for much more "mining" and reflection.

The Church

One of the most critical points in the theology of liberation is its reflection on Church. We are dealing here
with the internal, intra-ecclesial vector of this theology,
which seeks to express what the actual process of the base
Church communities posits concretely: a "new way of
being Church," that is, a new historical *process-and-project*
of Christian community.

This "new (way of being) Church" is identifiable by two
constitutive traits:

1. It is a *participatory Church*, in line with the emphasis
   on the people of God in *Lumen Gentium.* This means
   that, in the make-up of the Church, priority falls to
   baptism and the baptized. It means that each member of the Church is considered to be a living, active
   "ecclesial subject" (active agent of being-Church),
   actively sharing and participating in what it means to
   be Church. Pastors and clergy, here, come second.
   They are in a subordinate position; they are the
   servants of the people of God and the inspirers of
   their faith, hope, and love.
2. The Latin American Church is a *church of liberation*, in
   keeping with the emphasis on a "Church in the

world" seen in *Gaudium et Spes*. In our case it will be a "Church in the sub-world" of the poor, espousing their cause, taking flesh in their popular milieux, being the leaven of prophecy and justice and the seed of a new social order.

These emphases or significations are posited, as always, from a starting point in the unquestioned basis of a global view of the Church as the expression of the Divine Mystery. Indeed, it is in the light of this mystery of Church that these historical dimensions of faith come to expression in our theology.

Other Theological Themes

We could go on to show how the theology of liberation sets in relief, explores the concrete dimensions of, still other theological themes. In *moral theology,* for example, the notions of "social sin" and "social love" enjoy a special importance. Liberation morality is a morality of the Beatitudes in a political context, as the spirit of nonviolence, love of neighbor, and so on.

Each theme of theology has a special, concrete resonance in Latin American society.

Spirituality

Before concluding this part of our discussion we should like to broach one more instance of a Latin American approach to a traditional theme of Christian faith. It may well be in *spirituality* that liberation theology has produced its most valid and useful reflection. Nor should this be any cause for astonishment, since the *ultimate root of the theology of liberation is of a mystical order: the encounter with God in the poor.* After all, the spirit of liberation theology is expressed in key notions such as the following, which impregnate and propel the liberating commitment of the oppressed, and of those who struggle at their side.

- *Conversion* to the poor and to evangelical poverty.

- A *communion* of sisters and brothers in a committed community.

- *Hope* in a kingdom of God in history in the form of a new society.

- *Service* to and with the oppressed.

- *Incarnation* among and *solidarity* with the outcast.

- *"Parrhesia"*—the prophetic courage and freedom of proclamation and denunciation.

- *Patience* along the historical byways of a people in the wilderness of the world.

- The *cross* of persecution and martyrdom, in the footsteps and discipleship of Jesus Christ.

7

CONTRIBUTIONS
AND ACHIEVEMENTS

Let us now attempt a kind of summing-up of the merits, or more modestly, the contributions to the Church and the larger society, of the theology of liberation. It will be a precarious undertaking, inasmuch as these merits and contributions are matters of a very recent past, and especially of an ongoing present. Some are specific to the theology of liberation, while others are simultaneously the contribution of the actual communities with which liberation theology is linked.

To have called attention to the existence of the poor and to their quest for liberation

Liberation theology has sought only to interpret and articulate the cry, so often stifled, of the oppressed, and to bestow on their faith praxis its title of theological legitimacy. The theology of liberation has succeeded in reminding the Church of the suffering of the poor, and of their call to this Church for conversion and solidarity.

Liberation theology has made no attempt to usurp the function of the poor themselves, in a spirit of paternalism, in making this contribution, but only seeks in all modesty to strengthen and add to their voices and their faith, as it acknowledges them to be the primary agents of their own liberation.

To have made an essential contribution to the liberative meaning of Christian faith

The theology of liberation has been the theoretical reflex. and reflection of our communities' refutation in actual practice of the allegation that religion is the opium of the people—demonstrating that, in the Churches of Latin America, religion can be and is a leaven of justice. In this wise it has set forth the conception of a *prophetic* or *messianic* religion, as religion appears in its original biblical form. The notion of an *ideological religion,* then—a "mystifying religion," one which consecrates the status quo—has been deprived of its specious normativity once and for all.

To have expressed and legitimated the demand for a popular fabric of Church

Liberation theology has led the Church to take the poor seriously, procuring their recognition as *among the primary ecclesial agents* and the repositories of a particular "evangelizing potential," in the words of Puebla (Puebla Final Document, no. 1147).

To have conceived of theology as "second act" vis-à-vis the first act of the concrete life and practice of faith

Liberation theology's conception of theology as consequent upon faith practice has forced theologians to listen to the poor, has led them to enter into the faith community of their sisters and brothers, has induced them to relativize their function, thereby demystifying their image.

To have shifted the principal locus of the theological endeavor from academe (the department, the institute, the seminary) to the church community itself.

The theologian's first place is at the heart of the faith

community, in order to be of service to that community as it endeavors to face its challenges. Liberation theology has learned, and therefore teaches, that theology is always done in contact with the living community.

Not the least of the merits of the theology of liberation is to have conferred upon theology a particularly profound and concrete ecclesial reality, by doing theology in communion with the pastors of the living Christian communities.

To have assigned the theologian the special task of "thinking concrete praxis," of thinking the real problems of the community of faith, instead of abstract issues bereft of a connection with the life of God's people

The theology of liberation has always sought to manifest deep roots in reality, especially in the reality that constitutes the life of the poor—who are the vast majority of human beings living in Latin America—and never disappearing behind the clouds of a disincarnate spiritualism.

To have moved theology closer to the people, and made it "everybody's business"—not just the "business" of theologians, but that of simple people as well

This effort to "popularize theology" has encountered and lent reinforcement to a correlative phenomenon: the emergence of a "popular theology," developed by the Christian community itself in its capacity as primary theological agent. After all, the people of God, who profess their faith, *also have the right to think their faith*, and the professional theologian can encourage and support them in this undertaking. This is how the theology of liberation seeks to be of service to them.

Thus theology has initiated a process of "declericalization," so that it ceases to constitute the monopoly of specialists—although, paradoxically, the latter now become even more necessary than they were before, precisely by reason of their new task.

To have given theology a public character and weight

This was inevitable as soon as theology resolved to pay serious attention to the great problems of social groups. Hence the involvement and interest of these groups in the theology of liberation.

To have undertaken a forthright assimilation of the positive contributions of the social sciences

The theology of liberation has the merit of having shifted the focus until recently enjoyed by philosophy as cultural mediation for theology, to the area of the social sciences, seeing that the latter present more adequate credentials as suppliers of information about the questions this theology has to face. After all, the questions are social questions.

To have confronted the question of Marxism from a new locus—no longer a cultural one (as in the Christian-Marxist dialogue), but from a starting point in the real situation of the poor (a situation of oppression-and-liberation)

Marxism can be used by liberation theologians only as a simple means of service to a higher cause—the poor and their integral liberation. From these poor as a starting point—that is, from a point of departure in actual reality and praxis—the theoretical project of Marxism is judged, re-created, and transformed by theology.

We could go on to speak of spirituality, ecumenism, preparation for the priesthood, and so on. But surely the indications we have given will be more than sufficient to exemplify the merits, or contributions, of this new theology.

8

SOME CONCRETE CHALLENGES AHEAD

Liberation theology is a theology in its infancy. It has a great deal of growing to do. It needs to have its personality more clearly shaped, better defined. It has other challenges ahead of it, too—not its own exclusively, to be sure, but the ones it will have to face along with the whole Latin American Church, with whose becoming it is organically linked.

Following are three of the most important challenges looming for tomorrow.

A clearer explication of the centrality and sovereignty of faith in a reflection on the people's concrete praxis

It is not that the theology of liberation is particularly exposed to the danger of losing its evangelical identity for want of ascribing a clearly central position to faith. Rather, this theology is challenged to demonstrate this evangelical identity in depth, in the focus of a historical task and within that historical task. Liberation theology is in a particularly favorable position for this demonstration, living as it does in such immediate contact with the community that professes and celebrates this faith. And this is all the more the case for the fact that this community is composed so very preponderantly of the poor, among whom the faith dimension is more keenly felt and more tellingly expressed.

Still, on the theoretical level, the theology of liberation must improve its "epistemological profile," its theoretical status, as well as articulate its discourse in more consistent fashion, in such a way as to correspond more adequately to the praxis of the total Church community.

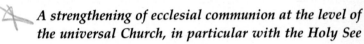

A strengthening of ecclesial communion at the level of the universal Church, in particular with the Holy See

To this purpose it will be crucial to keep channels of communication open, so that frank dialogue may dissolve ignorance and clarify misunderstandings.

Given the nature of liberation theology—its consubstantiality with a determinate ecclesial process—a sharing of experience, through visits between authorities of the universal Church and those of the local and regional churches, will be of the highest urgency.

A resumption of the dialogue with the theologians of other churches, on the basis of a fundamental equality

Born and bred in Latin America, the theology of liberation nevertheless is, and seeks only to be, "catholic," in the theological sense of the word. It cannot, therefore, close itself off from an encounter with the theologies of other churches, in an attitude of defensiveness, polemics, or reversed colonialism.

It will be of the utmost moment for the theology of liberation always to maintain a spirit of self-criticism, eschewing all false security and triumphalism.

There is no need for this theology to seek an escape, either from the discharge of its own task or from an examination of the task undertaken by others, with a view to mutual correction and enrichment.

What are the "theological gifts" of liberation theology to this communion, in von Balthasar's sense? The esteemed European theologian Hans Urs von Balthasar put it this way: "Here in South America something absolutely central to Christianity is emerging: the option for the poor. This is now part and parcel of Christianity" (*30 Giorni*, June 1984, p. 78).

This, then, is our first "gift." It is on the level of *content:* the *option for the poor*, that central element of the faith that the Church and the theology of Latin America have plucked from oblivion, to the advancement of the Gospel of the poor and the poor of the Gospel.

As the *Instruction* itself declared to all theologians without exception: "We must not become oblivious, be it for a single instant, of the situation of excruciating misery that lies at the root of this challenge to theologians" (chap. 4, no. 1).

"South American theologians," von Balthasar continued, "tell us that we do theology too theoretically, with our heads a bit in the clouds." And this brings us to the second "theological gift" from Latin America. This time it is in the area of *method:* the *doing of theology from a starting point in practice.*

This, then, is the "new word" spoken by the theology of liberation—a theology of the people and a theology in its infancy—to the venerable theology of the West: "For the poor, from within practice."

Clodovis Boff

II

Dialogue

9

OBSERVATIONS ON
THE PUBLICATION OF
THE *INSTRUCTION*

The *Instruction on Certain Aspects of the "Theology of Liberation"* was the fruit of a reflection carried on entirely within the Congregation.* It is known on direct authority of the highest sources in the Vatican that there had been no previous consultation with the national Bishops' Conferences of Latin America or with the Latin American Bishops' Conference. Hence the document's peculiar outlook, one foreign to the milieu where the theology in question originated, flourishes, and is being practiced. Nor indeed was any draft shown to the presidents of the various Latin American Bishops' Commissions for Doctrine on the occasion of their meeting with the authorities of the Congregation for the Doctrine of the Faith in Bogotá in April 1984. Initially the document was to have been limited to a consideration of the relationship between Marxist analysis and theology. But when the text was presented to the Holy

---

* The original text furnished by the Brazilian Nunciature was in Portuguese (Brazilian Portuguese, whereas all other pontifical documents have been sent to us in the Portuguese of Portugal), French, and Latin. A résumé was distributed in Spanish, to be published, and this had all the earmarks of an apocryphal document: it was unsigned, bore no seal of any Roman congregation, and included no protocol. Moreover, it was a poor summary of the *Instruction*, as it placed undue emphasis on the negative elements of the latter. Many bishops distributed only this summary. Many others protested to the Nunciature that the summary was an unacceptable distortion of the *Instruction*.

Father, who always has the last word in matters of doctrine, he found it to be too purely negative and returned it to the Congregation for amplification and greater balance. Thus the original text became chapter 7 of the document in its present form, and new material was added, which would "place in evidence," as Pope John Paul II had requested, "in a positive way, all of the wealth, as well for doctrine as for practice," of the theology of liberation (*Instruction*, Intro.). In fact, the Pope prescribed that an initial portion of the document would clearly set forth the following positive elements: liberation as an aspiration of whole peoples, now come to urgent expression (and we have this in chapters 1 and 2 of the document as it exists in its final form); liberation as an authentically Christian theme and concept (chap. 3); its basis in the Bible (chap. 4); and the voice of the magisterium in its regard (chap. 5). Thus the Sovereign Pontiff sought to emphasize the positive import of liberation theology as a "perfectly valid expression, designating, in this case, a theological reflection centered on the biblical theme of liberation and freedom, and on the urgency of their implementation in practice" (chap. 3, no. 4). And indeed, as this citation indicates, the theology of liberation represents the convergence of the peoples' aspirations for liberation and freedom with the biblical theme of freedom and liberation. A consistent articulation between the discourse of faith and the discourse upon reality requires and thereby justifies the theology of liberation—guarantees the validity of such a thing.

The Vatican document does not come to us with the authority of a papal encyclical, nor even with that of an apostolic exhortation (such as *Evangelii Nuntiandi*) but was published as an "instruction" of the Congregation for the Doctrine of the Faith. As such it has the approval of the

Holy Father, just as do other documents issued by Roman congregations; but it does not engage the whole of the ordinary magisterial authority of the Pope. Furthermore, in view of the document to be issued later—officially promised by the present *Instruction*—it can scarcely be considered to be the "last word" of the doctrinal authorities of the Church. At the same time, of course, it merits all the respect that is due to the official source that issued it.

The Vatican document was accepted by all concerned. At the same time, it was quick to provoke a reaction in the form of public qualifications of its statements by certain respected cardinals. The effect of this was to soften the harshness of the document and de-fang it of what otherwise could have been manipulated by the oppressors. This would have discouraged Christians committed to the liberation of the oppressed. Even Cardinal Ratzinger, Prefect of the Congregation for the Doctrine of Faith, in a discussion with reporters on the occasion of the official promulgation of the *Instruction* at the Vatican Printing Office, acknowledged that Marxism contains "certain valid, useful elements, but a much greater degree of vigilance, and a much more conscious criticism, are in order" than that which might need to be exercised vis-à-vis any other non-Christian system (*Osservatore Romano*, December 3–4, 1984, p. 4). The Cardinal Archbishop of Milan, Carlo Maria Martini, in a declaration over Vatican Radio, called for the exercise of a spiritual discernment regarding the theology of liberation, in the sense of "distinguishing its genuine, promising expressions from its ambiguous ones," and emphasizing that "the theology of liberation means encouragement for the oppressed," so that one must not "discourage, but enlighten and encourage all of those who, especially in Latin America, bring [the theology of liberation] to genuine expression, often with a fine spirit of sacrifice" (*La Repubblica*, September 9–10, 1984, p. 5). Cardinal Godfried Daneels, Archbishop of Malines-Brussels, upon his return from a pastoral visit to Latin America, expressed apprehension about what the secondary effects of the *Instruction* might be.

It is painful to see theologians blacklisted and their credibility harmed. The grassroots pastoral ministry suffers. Bishops ought to be encouraging those who work in this ministry. There is something tragic in all this, after so much effort, with such encouraging initial results. . . . Suffering can be salutary, but we should not aggravate it. . . . We ought to be showing our support for the poor and their theologians. [Interview in *De Standaard*, September 12, 1984]

The President of the Association of Roman Congregations, Secretary of State Cardinal Casaroli, made it clear that the Vatican's *Ostpolitik*, its relations with communist countries, would continue to be maintained, despite the document's position that socialism as it actually exists is "the shame of our time." He recently admitted that he had not been present at the ordinary session of the Congregation for the Doctrine of the Faith when the Instruction had been approved. He likewise expressed the opinion that it would have been preferable to begin the literature with a document in a positive tone rather than with this negative one (*L'Unità*, October 19, 1984).

In Brazil, Cardinal Aloísio Lorscheider, with his profound sense of balance and ecclesial communion, while acknowledging the valid elements in the *Instruction*, did not delay in raising questions calculated to be conducive to a more complete understanding of liberation theology, to the benefit of the oppressed and of the Church itself—

which latter, in the light of the Gospel, seeks to be the agent of deliverance and liberation. Cardinal Lorscheider expressed the hope that the more positive document, promised in the present *Instruction,* would strengthen and deepen this understanding (*Revista Eclesiástica Brasileira,* December 1984).

In the conversation held by Cardinals Joseph Ratzinger, Paulo Evaristo Arns, Aloísio Lorscheider, the Secretary of the Congregation for the Doctrine of the Faith Bishop Bovone, and myself (Leonardo Boff), on the occasion of my summons to that doctrinal office on September 7, 1984, the question of the new document was broached directly and the positive elements of liberation theology cited. Cardinal Arns, with the support of Cardinal Lorscheider, emphatically stated that in order to improve upon the *Instruction,* three basic things would have to happen. First, the "engineers" of the theology of liberation, the theologians who have been reflecting and writing on the subject for all these years (naming Gustavo Gutiérrez, Jon Sobrino, and the brothers Boff), ought to be invited to participate in preparing the new document.

Second, the episcopates, the bodies of bishops whose pastoral work is acknowledged as one of popular liberation, should be consulted in order to stress the pastoral and ecclesial character of the theology of liberation.

Third, a Third World site for the meeting should be selected—in Africa or Latin America, for instance—where bishops and theologians could see oppression firsthand and be present to the church communities and Christian groups who live a faith committed to liberation and life. This would create the necessary atmosphere for the development of a genuine theology of liberation and would take full account of the experience, theoretical and practical, of the churches. Then, faithful to the road already traversed, this theology would be able to universalize for the whole Church what the Spirit is stirring up on the world's periphery, in the churches of the poor.

With this habitual reticence and hesitancy, and citing certain difficulties he perceived, Cardinal Ratzinger nevertheless expressed his inclination to accept all three recommendations.

IS THERE A GENUINE, OFFICIAL LIBERATION THEOLOGY?

Despite its crucial limitations, the *Instruction* does cite certain positive elements in the theology of liberation, which must therefore now be considered solidly established for anyone proposing to work in that theology. First among these is the collective nature of the oppression that is stirring its victims to their longing for liberation. This is a basic biblical and magisterial theme. A reflection that will take both poles into account—the reality of oppression with the thirst for liberation on the one hand, and the data of revelation on the other—will be legitimate and valid in liberation theology. This is an important statement, in view of the campaign of vilification of which the theology of liberation has been the recent victim at the hands of theologians and Church authorities alike, especially on the part of the old leadership of the Latin American Bishops' Conference.

Second, the *Instruction* calls on Christians to make a firm commitment to the struggle for justice and liberation. The document rejects the specious distinction, adduced even in Brazil, between "theocentricity" and "anthropocentricity," or between persons concerned for orthodoxy and those committed to the liberation of the poor. The *Instruction* is altogether explicit here, and makes an appeal to theologians of all hues: "We must never forget, not even for an instant, the crying misery that is at the root of this challenge to theologians" (chap. 4, no. 1). In closing, the document insists that "there can be no concern for the purity of the faith without a concern to offer the response of an efficacious witness of service to one's neighbor, especially the poor and oppressed, through a life that is integrally 'theological,'" integrally the divine life of grace (chap. 11, no. 18).

Neither pietism nor secularism will be in order, then, but rather a confrontation of oppression with the light of the Gospel, yielding the urgency of liberation—a confrontation of faith with poverty, yielding a preferential option for the poor, and expressed in solidarity with them.

Finally, liberation, for Christians, draws its inspiration from the Gospel, in the "truth about Christ, the Church, and the human being" (chap. 11, no. 5). Marxism may never be allowed to become a determinative reference point and principle (chap. 8, no. 1). If Marxism is understood as a closed, monolithic system, denying God, the dignity of the person, and human freedom and rights, as the *Instruction* presents it (chap. 7, nos. 6,9), then obviously a theologian may not utilize it as a conceptual tool for understanding history and the conflicts of history, as such a system would stand in diametrical opposition to Christianity. (Of course, we might question what competency the Church enjoys to define Marxism or any other social system.)

We might ask, however, whether any theologian actually accepts Marxism in the totality to which the *Instruction* refers. In all frankness, we must admit that, in all our years of theological work, in the course of which we have made the acquaintance of practically all the principal theologians of liberation, we have never encountered such a theoretical and practical monstrosity. A Christian openness to the human, a Christian acceptance of the concrete transcendency of history and of each human person, will constrain us to reject Marxist totalitarianism, especially in its Stalinist version. To cast general aspersions on liberation theologians' use of certain select categories of Marxist analytical tradition as tantamount to a "denial of the faith in practice" (chap. 6, no. 9)—as tantamount to a denial of faith in the Incarnate Word (chap 20, no. 11), in the redemptive character of his death (no. 12), in the sacramentality of the Church (no. 15), and in the sacrament of the Eucharist as the sacramental presence of Christ's atoning sacrifice (no. 16), is to accuse these theologians of implicit heresy, by which they would be placing themselves effectively outside the faith community. But liberation theologians, by their involvement in the process of the liberation of the poor and oppressed, the vast majority of whom are Christians on our continent, or by their activity in their local Churches, precisely testify, through their life and option, to the truth of the faith. For the highest ecclesiastical authorities to defame and calumniate them in this underhanded way is intolerable. And the same defamation is practiced when liberation theologians are accused of being dupes and dreamers and fomenters of class struggle who are closed to dialogue—ivory-tower academics, then, instead of persons immersed in the situations of misery and oppression that constitute the life of the poor. No, liberation theologians promote armistice, not conflict. They are the heralds of resistance in the name of the Gospel, not lovers of division in society and the Church.

Such unjust accusations betray ignorance and the absence of any dialogue with those episcopates that are engaged in authentic Christian work among the people. They betray an ignorance of the literature of the theology of liberation, which, though written in the Latin American languages, is now translated into practically every Western tongue.

A consideration of these dimensions would have enabled the Congregation to avoid the gaping lacunae in the *Instruction*—omissions all the more painful for the crucial gaps they leave in their description and assessment of liberation theology's practice and understanding of the faith. The document has not one word about the movement of spirituality that has provided liberation theology with its actual matrix, or about the persecution and martyrdom of so many Christians—Archbishop Oscar Arnulfo Romero of San Salvador, Bishop Angelelli in Argentina, priests, sisters, brothers, and countless pastoral ministers and committed lay people of our Christian communities, as well as the anonymous indigenous Christian peasants inspired by the Gospel, and cut down as they attempted to defend their culture and their lands. None of this can be seen to bode very well for Church communities where the faithful experience a synthesis of Gospel and life.

Passing over other shortcomings in the Roman document, let us observe some positive elements to be underscored in a perspective of a more comprehensive and more just assessment of the theology of liberation.

Twice (chap. 11, nos. 4, 12) the document summons theologians to dialogue and collaboration in the face of new questions which could enrich the social teaching of the Church. In view of this invitation, and primarily with an eye to this positive, in-depth collaboration, we presume to suggest some avenues for reflection.

11

STARTING POINT:
THE LIGHT OF FAITH AND
THE PROCESSES OF OPPRESSION
AND LIBERATION

As heirs of the original Gospel teaching, Christians experience their concrete oppression as a scandal, and contrary to the will of God. In recent years, after so many centuries of resistance to and dismantling of popular movements, a liberation process has developed at the roots of society. A critical awareness has suddenly sprung up, manifested in an effort to share in society and in politics, expressed in the creation of popular movements (unions, neighborhood associations, Amerindian organizations, associations of landless peasants), claiming rights and demanding changes in the form of a greater participation in societal and political structures, all in the name of justice. This historical and social bloc of oppressed people extends far beyond Marx's classic "proletariat" and includes even influential elements in the Church—cardinals, bishops, members of religious orders, the diocesan clergy, and the vast network of base church communities and Bible study groups. A commitment to the poor and to necessary changes in society is felt as an urgent matter of faith. Base-community problems, neighborhood problems, and the problems of society as a whole are all challenges to this commitment. A genuine process of liberation from the reality of oppression is under way.

When we speak of liberation, we are not referring, as the *Instruction* does, to a theme of Scripture or church tradition as one might look up a word in the dictionary. Liberation to us means a concrete, historical route, traced by the oppressed themselves together with their allies, with its defeats, its partial victories, and the immense capacity for sustained resistance, in faith, hope, and love that flows from the Christian message. We are dealing with something here that is far more real than the type of discourse maintained in the *Instruction* concerning "liberation and aspirations thereto." Aspirations, yes, but aspirations become fact and deed! Never shall we attain to real liberation merely by fostering "aspirations" to the same— any more than we shall feed the hungry by reading kitchen recipes to them. The biblical theme of liberation and freedom is basic to an understanding of the people of God of the Old and New Testaments, or even of the actions of Jesus himself. But reflection on all this is not enough. Christians have been meditating the Scriptures for two thousand years, thus maintaining constant contact with the scriptural theme of liberation and freedom. And there are still poor and outcast among us. The "urgency of practical incidences" proclaimed by the *Instruction* does not automatically produce these practical incidences, all idealistic illusions to the contrary notwithstanding. Hell is paved with good intentions. "Good ideas" do not work *ex opere operato*. Liberation, as the structure of the word suggests, is an *action*, and it consists in the act of liberating captive freedom. Liberation activity can receive illumination and support from the "thematics" of liberation, but they cannot replace it.

12

THE AGENTS OF LIBERATION:
THE OPPRESSED
AND THEIR ALLIES

The Church's preferential option for solidarity with the poor implies that it is the poor themselves, "conscientized and organized," who must become the primary agents and operators of their own liberation. The Church joins ranks with them in their struggles and their journey and has a specific contribution to make to their cause. Indeed, not only the Church, but all persons without exception of whatever social class, are called upon to take a position of solidarity with the poor and to work right alongside them in this high endeavor. No meaningful social change in history has ever been effected by one solitary segment of society but has always emerged from a concrete, historical alliance of a plurality of such segments. A pedagogy of the last twenty years developed by Paulo Freire has taught us all about a "pedagogy *of* the oppressed" (not *for* the oppressed), and about "education as the practice of freedom" (not as a "taming" process to facilitate the assimilation of the oppressed into the prevailing system). The poor are not only needy; they are exploited. Their capacity for creativity is immense in terms of values and culture, labor and social welfare. The oppressed have a power in history and a power for history—a power for evangelization, as Puebla humbly recognizes (Puebla Final Document, no. 1147).

It is most regrettable that the *Instruction* has not a single word to say on the glorious and powerful deeds of the poor. Nowhere in the document is there any reference to their organizations, their struggles, their advance, nor a solitary word of encouragement and support for their cause, for their collisions with the mighty oppressor, and for their lives. On the contrary, the whole document is shot through with the anachronism of paternalism and "assistentialism," with allusions to "the concern [of the Church] *for* the poor, and *for* the victims of oppression" (chap. 3, no. 3), the praiseworthy activity of Christians who "seek to assist and relieve the numberless ills that are the fruit of [their] misery" (chap. 6, no. 1), or the struggle "on behalf of the poor" (chap. 11, nos. 11, 13). We could have hoped for something more along the lines of Medellín and Puebla, which spoke not of a Church *for* the poor, in a spirit of paternalism, but of a Church *with* the poor, in a spirit of solidarity—and even of the Church *as* the poor, or a Church *with* the poor, in a spirit of identification (cf. Pope John Paul II, *Laborem Exercens*, no. 8). In Brazil, Pope John Paul II insisted with the poor: "You can be sure you will be helped. But do not abdicate your own capacities. Do everything possible to overcome that evil called poverty, with its retinue of other ills" (*Pronunciamentos do Papa no Brasil*, no. 776). Of the wealthy the Pope asked an effective option for the poor, and of the poor an option for other poor, or for the still poorer.

To the eyes of the Vatican *Instruction*, the poor seem to be outside the Church, whereas, as we know, in Latin America the poor are all but one hundred percent Christian. The Church undertakes a task of "aid," thereby seeking to "liberate" the poor without taking any account of their power in history or of their indispensable coopera- tion to the extent of their conscientization, their organiza- tion, and their active involvement.

Only a Church itself free and liberated from the histor- ical paternalism by which, surely without intending it, it has maintained the poor in a condition of dependency will truly help Christ's poor in their efforts to obtain their liberation. In union of solidarity with all of those who, under other inspiration, likewise go in quest of life, bread, and dignity, these Christian poor, because of their faith, undertake the same quest. More and more we ob- serve this phenomenon of the Spirit—that the hierarchy of the Church penetrates this continent of poor, heartening communities of Christians, Bible groups, and groups or- ganized for the promotion and defense of human life. And lo, a genuinely popular, liberative profile of the Church begins to take shape.

13

THE PRACTICE OF
LIBERATION AS STARTING
POINT FOR REFLECTION

The specific difference of liberation theology, among the sundry theological currents of our day, consists precisely in its endeavor to think the totality of the faith from a point of departure in the practice of liberation. Our theologians do not hole up in their academic departments preparing young men for the priesthood and composing tomes. They are closely involved with the grassroots groups, with the base church communities, with Bible groups, with human-rights centers, with seminars for lay ministers, priests, and bishops. They are frequently invited to serve as chaplains and advisors in the base groups (neighborhood associations, Christian Workers, slum associations, Black Unity and Black Awareness, associations for domestics, women's defense, and so on) for there are many practicing Christians in these groups, and the Church, through its pedagogy and its lines of action and reflection, has a contribution to make to the (nonpartisan) solution of social problems. Many theologians divide their time between academic work and the pastoral ministry. They plunge into the actual situation of poor Christians, sharing their lives, their cause, and their struggles, reflecting with them, selecting study topics with them, praying and working with them.

The theology of liberation starts with this type of Christian liberation practice. How should we "think God" and the highest mystery of the Most Holy Trinity in a context of popular practice? How should we be proclaiming Jesus Christ in a poor Christian milieu possessed of an acute awareness of injustice and banded together for the abolition of such-and-such particular oppressive practices? How should we live and celebrate the sacraments, along the pathway of community pilgrimage toward social change in the light of faith? What image of Church should we be creating and fostering so that the Church, as sacrament of Christ in the world, may be the vessel of the liberating memory of Jesus Christ, whose option was for the poor, who was never indifferent in the face of human oppression (sorrow, hunger, sin), who was persecuted for his new message, who died in consequence of his message and of the practice he was inaugurating, and who was raised from the dead to demonstrate the realization of the Father's plan which is eternal life for "the whole human being and all human beings"?

It is in the practice of liberation from concrete, historical oppression that Christians will discover the ever-present liberative dimensions of the Christian message. As M.-J. Scheeben said, all the Christian mysteries, even that of the Most Holy Trinity, are sacramental mysteries. That is, all are joined to some historical reality. In like manner we may say that the whole content of faith, as of each of its elements, is, in its own fashion, liberative. Neither faith nor any of its elements needs a superadded dimension of liberation accruing to it from without, adventitious to its intrinsic structure. This dimension is already present. It needs only to be extracted from within, where it is often obscured by a reductionistic practice of a hobbled, abridged reflection. God is, and always will be, the One before whom, like Moses of old, we must cover our face and adore the mystery (see Exodus 3:6).

But at the same time, this transcendent God, inhabiting light inaccessible (1 Timothy 6:16), is a God who abides with the oppressed, for he has heard their cry and decided upon their deliverance (Exodus 3:7–8). Here is revealed a God who "takes sides," who abominates the relations of oppression maintained by Pharaoh, and who joins in the liberation aspirations and practices of the oppressed slaves (Exodus 3:17, 19–20). In like fashion, Mary, as Paul VI explains, while surely "utterly abandoned to the Lord's will, is yet far from being a passive, submissive woman, but is a woman who does not hesitate to declare God to be the avenger of the lowly and oppressed of the earth, who casts down the mighty from their thrones and exalts the lowly [Luke 1:52], . . . the 'valiant woman' familiar with poverty and suffering, flight and exile—the situations that can escape the notice of no one who seeks to contribute, in the spirit of the gospel, to the *liberative* energies of the human being and of society" (*Marialis Cultus*, no. 37). There is no question, surely, of a "reductionistic reading of Scripture" in the Pope's theology—to recall the *Instruction's* complaint. The Holy Father is simply acknowledging the relevance of a dimension of the Bible to a situation in which the vast majority of Christians are suffering poverty and oppression. On the contrary, a refusal to accord the Magnificat its validity for today would be to reduce God's living word to a pool of stagnant waters.

Commitment to liberation implies a denunciation of situations in society and the Church that are displeasing to God, such as hunger, the premature death of thousands of children, subhuman working conditions, economic exploitation, military repression, and the manipulation of Christianity for the maintenance of these conditions, with the connivance of Church authorities who limit the concept of evangelization to the strictly intra-ecclesial, "religious" sphere, as if there were no sin, no love, no conversion, and no forgiveness in the social and political areas of society (see Puebla Final Document, no. 515; *Evangelii Nuntiandi*, no. 34). In order to grasp the proportions of prevailing social inequities, theology needs an *ancilla* in the form of a theoretical lucidity that can be the product only of the social and human sciences, as it is these that demonstrate the functioning of the mechanisms of poverty and thus enable theology to decide what to label as social sin. It is not a matter of whether to accept contributions of Marxism, as we shall see below, but of understanding where we can obtain the wherewithal to demonstrate that the poverty of the masses "is in many cases the result of a violation of the dignity of labor" (*Laborem Exercens*, no. 8).

Christians seek liberation, but they seek a liberation deriving from their very faith, for it is this faith that leads them and stirs them to their liberation commitment. Indeed, otherwise their faith is the dead faith of the demons, who "believe . . . and shudder" in hell itself (James 2:19, 26).

The theology of liberation, before being a "movement of ideas" or the "generator of a commitment to justice," as the *Instruction* would have it (chap. 3, no. 3), is itself generated by an antecedent concrete commitment to the exalted struggle for justice. Liberation theology is "second word" that grows out of a first, primary, basic "word" of practice. It is not a theology primarily of "conclusions"—one concluding merely to the *will* to act—but is a theology fundamentally involving action itself: an action always driven and guided by faith and by the Gospel present in the life of a people at once oppressed and Christian. The concrete practice of liberation calls for something besides evangelical inspiration and theological reflection.

And this something is a pedagogical knowledge of how communities, in the light of faith, become truly free of their instincts of hatred and revenge, how they manage to "extroject" these mental schemata that they have internalized down through the centuries of their manipulation at the hands of a dominant society. You have to become acquainted with the mechanisms that distill injustice, you have to be able to reckon the strength of your own forces and that of your allies, you have to plan your reaction to the dominant system that is so stubborn when it comes to change. You have to know what specific contribution may be forthcoming from the side of the institutional Church, as well as from lay groups. You have to know how to maintain a Christian identity in the midst of the processes of conflict. You have to know how to pray and how to grow spiritually, on a community level, while immersed in commitments that weld Gospel and life. A theologian who "just knows theology" will end by not even knowing theology. In a perspective of liberation, he or she must acquire the art of interconnecting the data of faith and the course of the world, the spirit of the Gospel and the struggles of the poor.

The Vatican document seeks excellent ends—liberation and freedom. But it betrays an extreme penury of means in its neglect of the poor themselves and of their allies—their principal ally being the Church itself. To a people immersed in the practice of liberation carried out in their Christian communities, it is most offensive to have to hear, in the words of the *Instruction,* that "the base communities lack catechetical and theological preparation, as well as a capacity for discernment" (chap. 11, no. 5). These expressions betray only the superficiality of a judgment rendered by persons ignorant of how a Christian community works from the inside, or the huge pedagogical labor of these last twenty years with its consciousness-raising, rehabilitation of popular piety, appropriation of the Scriptures by the communities, and the repeated deepening of faith through meditation on the great themes of faith. Theologians, bishops, even cardinals not only teach the people but are taught by the people, and they emerge strengthened in their faith—and even, according to abundant testimonials, converted by the most radical and authentic forms of evangelical experience. A failure to recognize what the Spirit is doing among Jesus' younger brothers and sisters (see Matthew 25:40) is intolerable on the part of an authentic ecclesial mentality. Why does the Vatican document manifest no sensitivity to this *sensus fidelium*? Communion will be genuine only when those responsible for orthodoxy hear what God is saying through their poor sisters and brothers, and when the poor open themselves to what the teachers of the faith recommend for their pondering. This communion, this two-way apprenticeship, would have avoided tension, resistance, a feeling of not being understood, and a mistrust of a haughty, imposed "truth."

At all events, we are absolutely convinced of this: that it will be oppressed Christians themselves, committed to integral liberation in the spirit of the Gospel—a liberation not only from the slavery of sin, then, but from economic, political, and cultural oppression, as well—who will be the judges of the practical, real contribution that an official document from Rome can make to the quest for that life, that dignity, that bread, that love, and that grace that God wills, even here in history, for his sons and daughters.

Having set forth these basic premises for a correct approach to an understanding of the theology of liberation as lived and theorized in Latin America, surely it will be in order for us to devote some space to the crucial question of Marxism, as it is for this point that the Vatican document reserves its keenest attention and the brunt of its severity.

THE VATICAN DOCUMENT'S AMBIGUOUS APPROACH TO MARXISM

"No" to Marxism as a Closed Ideology

The sore point, the most critical part of the *Instruction*, is its approach to the relationship of the theology of liberation with Marxism. This is evident in the document's Introduction and body (chaps. 7–10) alike.

Here we must be somewhat minute and analytical. The great danger, according to the *Instruction*, is that the use of Marxism will lead Christians to "deviate" from the faith and precisely betray the cause of the poor (Intro.; chap. 2, no. 3). And it is with this point that we can learn a great lesson from the Roman document. Liberation may not be won at the price of faith. Accordingly, it is not by Marxism, taken as an integral, exhaustive, and exclusive ideology, that a genuine liberation of the oppressed can be achieved. "Socialism in actual practice" is here before our eyes to demonstrate this, as the *Instruction* reminds us (chap. 11, no. 10). Christians will therefore eschew this alternative; to espouse it would be to scurry up a blind alley.

To be sure, then, we must struggle for justice. This is beyond all discussion (Intro.; chap. 4, no.1; chap.11). But, the document warns, the struggle must be waged from a point of departure in faith and in the transcendent inspiration of faith (chap. 11, no. 5; chap. 4).

This warning also obliges Christians to redouble their critical vigilance vis-à-vis Marxism, whose devouring mystical seduction is totalitarian here, and extremely difficult for incautious, uncritical minds to resist. At the same time, Christians are enjoined to seek ever deeper evangelical roots for their partisan social commitment to the poor.

Marxism as a "Steel Block"

But this is not all there is to say. We have seen only the negative side of the picture. The *Instruction* itself promises a richer, more positive "later document" (Intro.). This would be the constructive, positive side of the picture.

Inasmuch as theologians have been invited to a "collaboration" and "dialogue" (chap. 11, nos. 4, 12), we should like to register some reservations here. Indeed we must observe that the document's own view of the crucial question of Marxism is not as homogenous as it would like to have us believe. It is ambiguous. On the one hand it states that Marxism is an indivisible "block of steel," whose elements are mutually "indissociable" (chap. 7, no. 6; chap. 8, no. 2), so that it constitutes a "system in the strict sense" (chap. 9, no. 1), a "philosophico-ideological superstructure" (chap. 7, no. 6).

On the other hand the *Instruction* repeatedly calls for a "critical" attitude toward Marxism with regard to *some* of the elements borrowed from it by certain "theologies of liberation."

As to Marxism as an indivisible whole: The document seems to us to lend exaggerated credit to historical, classical Marxism's discourse upon itself. It seems to rest content with reading the label on the bottle rather than pulling the cork. Historical or positive Marxism (de facto "marxology") is one thing; actual theoretical Marxism, as a theory of social analysis, something else again. Where Marxism in the latter sense is concerned, neither the profession of faith on the part of the Soviet Academy of Sciences nor the horror expressed by the Congregation of the Doctrine of the Faith has any validity. This is not a question for authority. To consider it such would be to fall victim to a "theoretical authoritarianism" in which authority would simply decree what is scientific and what is not.

Further: The real facts about the Marxist system are irreconcilable with the analysis offered by the *Instruction*. In his apostolic letter *Octogesima Adveniens*, Pope Paul VI notes what he calls a veritable "explosion of Marxism" (no. 32) in various directions, while at the same time warning Christians of an "intimate link" between the "various elements" of Marxism and their original ideological matrix (no. 34). Even here the Pontiff was less rigid than the *Instruction*. We need only examine the terms of his warning—vigorous, surely, and indeed taken up and repeated by the *Instruction* of the Congregation for the Doctrine of the Faith (chap. 7, no. 7)—to the effect that it would be "illusory and dangerous . . . to forget," or fail to "recognize" or "perceive the intimate link" alluded to. But his tone is not: "Do not handle! Do not taste! Do not touch!" (Colossians 2:21).

The document itself recalls Pope John XXIII's distinction in *Pacem in Terris* (no. 159) between "doctrines" and "historical movements." Then surely we must be able to dissociate Marxism's praxis from its theory. We need only glance at European Communism.

It would seem, then, that the *Instruction* is forcing the issue a bit when it stresses the "difficulty" or even "impossiblity" of "purifying" Marxism (Intro.), considering it "incompatible" with Christian faith. The document would seem to be making a blanket statement for safety's sake, with pastoral prudence in mind, or for the sake of safeguarding the transcendent, absolute value of faith. It is difficult to interpret it as a statement of theoretical truth. It is simply stressing a hierarchy of value. It can scarcely be interpreted as asserting a basic theoretical incompatibility between Marxism and Christian faith. We must also recall the statement of the former General of the Jesuits, Pedro Arrupe, in his celebrated letter on Marxist analysis. With reference to certain frankly atheistic ideological and philosophical premises, he wrote:

> Marxist analysis is not the only analysis to have an admixture of such elements. . . . Indeed, the social analyses customarily practiced in the liberal [capitalist] world imply a materialistic, individualistic worldview equally contrary to Christian values and attitudes.

It would have been much better balanced of the *Instruction* to cite our world of liberal capitalism as well, as this is the economic system that has given rise to the various theologies of liberation by functioning as principal cause of the concrete, historical oppression of our people. Puebla pronounces this system a system of "practical atheism" (Puebla Final Document, no. 546)—one that ignores God in practice, and one that is "clearly sinful" (ibid., no. 92).

The Other, More Traditional Voice of the *Instruction*

After all, the Roman document goes on to urge—in hushed tones, to be sure (and over ten times!)—a "critical" attitude toward Marxism—and not only rejecting Marxism en bloc, but also warning against borrowing its "concepts," "elements," and even "methods."

However, Cardinal Ratzinger himself, as we have noted, acknowledges that we shall find valid and useful elements in Marx's system, provided we exercise a critical caution in using them.

The Roman document takes account of the need for a socio-analytic mediation—an ancillary use of the natural and human sciences by theology—in order to achieve a "social transformation" (chap. 7, no. 3). Now, may this mediation be provided by Marxism? The document is ambiguous here. It emphasizes the negative. It goes on the attack. But it does not succeed in escaping references to the "critical" use of Marxism's "concepts," "elements," and "methods," which can only be understood as tantamount to a tacit concession to Marxism by the authors of the *Instruction.*

There is another difficulty. The *Instruction*'s understanding of "scientific" as "necessarily true" (chap. 8, no. 1) is scarcely abreast of the times. "Scientific," on the contrary, today designates something open to discussion, subject to ongoing critique and refutation—and in no way enjoying the "necessary" and "definitive" character attributed to it by the Roman document in the spirit of the scientific mythology of the nineteenth century.

Furthermore, the document's description of Marxism in its key chapters, which takes its starting point in the notion of "class struggle" conceived of as Marxism's "ideological nucleus" and "basic law of history," is an out-and-out caricature—as is the "pastoral Leninism" to which the document concludes from this imagined "nucleus." Simply to saddle liberation theology with "firing on the crowd to shoot the murderer" is to calumniate liberation theologians as practical deniers of the faith (chap. 6, no. 9).

Beyond Marxism

Whatever truth there is in Marxism—always a merely "approximative" truth, of course—Christian faith will always consider that truth to be something it must assimilate. In this, the attitude of faith toward Marxism is no different from its attitude toward any other system of thought. This is not "rehabilitation" or "theft" but simply the recovery of "goods already belonging" to the Christian faith in the first place, as Saint Augustine, along with so many other Church Fathers, insisted.

Pope John Paul II, in his encyclical *Redemptor Hominis* speaks in the same tenor, referring to the attitude, at once positive and critical, adopted by Christianity toward philosophical ideologies and systems all through history. And Saint Thomas Aquinas, rehearsing a principle already hoary with venerability, said: "Omne verum, a quocumque dicatur, a Spiritu Sancto est"—all truth, no matter who utters it, is from the Holy Spirit. Christian faith stubbornly refuses to believe that the "real light which gives light to every man" (John 1:9) has not beamed at least a little on every system of thought—Christianity refuses the notion that there could be a thought system utterly bereft of anything that could be liberated or saved.

Only if faith is right in this, of course, can Marxism really be transcended, really "gone through and gotten beyond"—entirely apart from the difficulty of calling the system "Marxism" at all, a patronymic that has become an annoying, anachronistic misnomer on several grounds: political, pastoral, pedagogical, and finally (and especially) theoretical. As to the theoretical inappropriateness of the epithet, we must recognize that no science or truth can be the private property of anyone at all, not even of its own "father." As for the political utilization of the label "Marxist" today, in many Latin American countries it is used to denounce someone as a "Communist" to the secret police. Archbishop Oscar Arnulfo Romero knew this and confided to the Pope: "Holy Father, it is very dangerous to speak of 'anti-communism' in my country. 'Anti-communism' is a right-wing slogan. It is affixed to people not out of love or Christian sentiments, but out of selfishness, to safeguard the user's own interests" (*Romero—y lo mataron* ["Romero—And They Killed Him"] [Rome: AVE, 1980], p. 162).

At the same time, the Christian communities and the bishops of Latin America do use "elements" borrowed from Marxism—without, for all that, being bound by its ideology or having to wear the Marxist label and tip their hats to Karl Marx. Pope John Paul II does much the same in many of his own messages, especially in his encyclical *Laborem Exercens*, where he uses, with perfect freedom and against a horizon of faith, categories he borrows from Marx: alienation, exploitation, means of production, dialectic, praxis, and so on (see *Laborem Exercens*, no. 11). Nor does anyone accuse him of Marxism on this account! As Karl Barth said long ago: "I can in all tranquillity allow elements of Marxism to enter my head without thereby becoming a Marxist." This is what we mean by going beyond Marxism—using Marxism as a stepping-stone to something further, in a dialectic of through-and-beyond.

The Symbol of the Obelisk in Saint Peter's Square

Finally, what the theology of liberation, like any theology, must have is a truly *catholic* spirit, a truly universal spirit. It must have a spirit of *integration*, not *integralism*, a spirit fully appreciative of the faith and hence of its power of assimilation. After all, Christianity has demonstrated all through history that it has an "ostrich's stomach"—that it can swallow anything, and transform it.

In the center of Saint Peter's Square in Rome stands an Egyptian obelisk. On its pinnacle is the cross of our redemption. It is an eloquent symbol of the assimilative power of the *Catholic* faith. No pilgrim to the Eternal City takes scandal at seeing this element of another religious system assimilated into the Christian symbolic system. And the inscription at the base of the obelisk explains why this need not be:

Sixtus V, Supreme Pontiff, did command that this Vatican obelisk, of old dedicated to the impious cult of pagan gods, be transported, despite the greatest difficulties, to this See of the Apostles.

And there it stands, at the very gates of the Vatican, and in the very center of Saint Peter's Square. Let us look and learn.

Leonardo Boff
Clodovis Boff

III

Confrontation

15

SUMMONS TO ROME:
A PERSONAL TESTIMONY

Antecedents

In 1981, Editora Vozes brought out my *Igreja: carisma e poder: Ensaios de eclesiologia militante* ("Church—Charism and Power: Essays in Militant Ecclesiology"), a collection of thirteen essays on various aspects of the Church, written during the fifteen years of my theological activity to date.

A polemical reaction to my book ensued. Dom Estêvão Bettencourt, o.s.b., wrote against it in *Pergunte e Responderemos*, January-February 1982, pp. 15–26. Friar Boaventura Kloppenburg, soon to be auxiliary bishop of Salvador, BA, published a critique in the review *Communio*, 1982, pp. 126–47, with the same article appearing in the Sunday edition of the newspaper *Jornal do Brasil* for June 27, 1982. The Archdiocesan Commission for the Doctrine of the Faith, headed by Bishop Karl Joseph Romer, assisted by Benedictine Father Estêvão Bettencourt and Father Ney de Sá Earp, reprinted, in *Boletim da Revista do Clero*, February 1982, pp. 26–30, a review by Urbano Zilles, stating, inter alia, that "[Boff] begins with the premise that the institutional Church as it exists today has no connection with the

Gospel, and contains only lies and illusions, so that it must be unmasked and 'demystified'" (ibid., p. 27). Here I judged that I must register a protest. My response to the Commission and to Zilles appeared in the April 1982 issue of the same *Boletim da Revista do Clero*, pp. 23–26, along with Zilles' rebuttal, pp. 27–29. I made another reply, but the *Boletim* refused to print it, and so I published it in *Grande Sinal*, June 1982, pp. 383–87, along with a response to Estêvão Bettencourt, pp. 388–99. Dom Romer concluded the discussion with an article in the *Boletim*, April 1982.

On February 2, 1982, I sent a copy of Zilles' critique, which had been adopted as the position of the Doctrinal Commission of Rio de Janeiro, along with my reply, to the Congregation for the Doctrine of the Faith in Rome. There, under date of April 14, Cardinal Ratzinger wrote to me acknowledging receipt of this material and asking me to furnish a reply to Boaventura Kloppenburg's article in *Communio* as well. This I did, and the reply appeared in the June issue of *Revista Eclesiástica Brasileira*, pp. 227–45. In the same issue, again, Father Carlos Palacio, s.j., published an analysis entitled, "Da polêmica ao debato teológico: a propósito do livro de L. Boff" ("From Polemic to Theological Debate: On the Book by Leonardo Boff"). The discussion appeared to be at an end.

Under date of May 15, 1984, through the Franciscan Superior General, Friar John Vaughn, o.f.m., Cardinal Ratzinger dispatched to me a six-page letter criticizing "not a few positions that are less than fully worthy of acceptance" in my book. His Eminence made two series of observations. The first concerned theological method. The second dealt with questions referring to (1) the structure of the Church, (2) the conception of dogma and revelation, and (3) the exercise of religious authority. Finally, the Cardinal

Prefect extended to me an invitation to hold a conversation with him in Rome in the coming months of June and July, adding: "In view of the influence the book has had on the faithful, this letter will be published, along with an indication of any position Your Reverence may see fit to adopt in the matter."

Cardinal Ratzinger's letter, dated May 15, arrived in Father General's hands only on May 28. In it His Eminence solicits the General's intervention in the affair, with a view to securing a "favorable attitude toward [these] observations" on my part and my "prompt reply" to his invitation to a "conversation" in Rome.

I received Cardinal Ratzinger's letter in Brazil only on June 16. On June 18 I sent him my acceptance of the invitation. I asked for a clarification of the nature of the "conversation"—whether it would be an official interchange, and hence subject to the norms spelled out in the Congregation's *Ratio Agendi* (that is, whether it would be a juridical proceeding) or whether it would be exempt from these norms. I requested that the members of the Brazilian Bishops' Commission on Doctrine, whose President was a cardinal and a theologian, Aloísio Lorscheider, be allowed to participate in the "conversation." I suggested that, in case the meeting could not be held in Brazil, it be held in Rome only in early October.

Under date of July 16, Cardinal Ratzinger replied that the conversation would be with himself and one other person only, who would accompany him, and that it would have to be held in Rome, since, "in conformity with the decisions taken, based on the *Ratio Agendi*, it would not appear to be possible to hold the conversation jointly with the Doctrinal Commission of the Brazilian Bishops' Conference."

The "conversation" was to be official, then. His Eminence designated "September 7 or 8" as the date for the meeting, remarking that no postponement was possible. He reiterated the intention of the Congregation to publish the six-page letter of criticisms to which I have referred. In a letter of August 8, I repeated my request to have the "conversation" held in Brazil, citing the principle of subsidiarity so strongly featured in the new Code of Canon Law and reiterated by Cardinal Ratzinger himself in his meeting with the Presidents of the national Bishops' Commissions for Doctrine in Bogotá and again in a public interview in Rome in April, 1984. I inquired what language the conversation would be held in, who would accompany the Cardinal Prefect of the Congregation to the meeting and be present during it, whether I would have access to the minutes of discussions held on the matter within the Congregation before my summons to Rome, and who would be responsible for travel expenses. I urged the Sacred Congregation not to proceed with its plan to publish the six-page letter before the "conversation" was held, as it contained erroneous citations both of the Holy Father and of my book, which would detract from the credibility of the august ecclesiastical authority represented by the Congregation for the Doctrine of the Faith.

On July 10 I met with Cardinal Primate of Brazil, Dom Avelar Brandão Vilela. His great prudence and wisdom have been of great help to me. Then I met with Dom Aloísio Lorscheider, Cardinal President of the Doctrinal Commission of the Brazilian Bishops' Conference, and with Cardinal Paulo Evaristo Arns, Archbishop of São Paulo, who had been my teacher, and who was still an inspiration and encouragement in my theological activity. Finally, on August 13 and 14, I had useful conversations in Brasilia with the President of the Brazilian Bishops' Conference. As this prelate, Dom Ivo Lorscheiter, was planning to visit the Apostolic See in September to discuss various matters of concern to the Brazilian church, we agreed that Cardinal Aloísio, President of the Brazilian Bishops' Doctrinal Commission, should be along; then, in Rome, Dom Ivo and Cardinal Aloísio would broach the possibility of their presence, as members of the Brazilian episcopate, at the "conversation" I would be holding with the Cardinal Prefect of the Sacred Congregation for the Doctrine of the Faith. Cardinal Paulo Evaristo Arns, too, manifested a desire to participate in the conversation, inasmuch as he would be passing through Rome about that time on his way to Germany and Poland.

At last, on August 30, the Apostolic Nuncio to Brazil, Dom Carlo Furno, in the name of the Congregation for the Doctrine of the Faith, served notice to me that the conversation would be held on September 8, in a language agreeable to all of the participants.

The Conversation with Cardinal Ratzinger in Rome

I arrived in Rome on September 2, 1984. I was literally assaulted by reporters, first as I left the plane, and then in the airport. My brother, Clodovis Boff, who was in Rome to teach at the Marian College (which he was later prevented from doing, in virtue of having been stripped of his *missio canonica* by Cardinal Eugênio Sales, Archbishop of Rio de Janeiro), was there to greet me, along with our sister, Sister Lina Boff, who had been working in the Eternal City for five years. My only statement to the reporters was: "I have come to Rome not as a pilgrim, not as a tourist, and not as a participant in a theological congress. I have come here in response to a summons by the Prefect of the Congregation for the Doctrine of the Faith. I shall have to answer his questions, not yours. I am in the Holy Father's diocese. Out of respect for him I shall speak only within the premises of the Sacred Congregation."

And I did indeed go into seclusion at the Franciscan headquarters, near the Vatican. Through my window I could see the huge cupola of Saint Peter's Basilica. From Sunday till Friday, the day of my conversation with Cardinal Ratzinger, I had no contact with anyone whatsoever outside the Franciscan headquarters, but busily prepared my responses to the theological questions that had been raised. I had already prepared, in Brazil, a fifty-page text, which had been read by the Franciscan cardinals, and in which, drawing upon the fonts of Church tradition, I sought to respond to the six pages drawn up by the Sacred Congregation.

September 3, 1985, saw the publication of *Instruction on Certain Aspects of the "Theology of Liberation."* The press regarded my presence in Rome and my "conversation" with Cardinal Ratzinger as the implementation of the criticisms leveled against liberation theology in the document—their application to the case of a particular theologian. It was front-page material, and I received hundreds of requests for interviews. I granted none, however; the Brother Porter deftly parried all requests and supplied the necessary explanations.

Likewise on September 3 I was visited by Cardinal Ratzinger's private secretary, Father Joseph Klemens. Father Klemens was accompanied by a theologian of the Sacred Congregation, Father Eugenio X. Aramburu. They were concerned about media reaction to my case, and about their allegation that the Sacred Congregation was resurrecting methods in disuse for years now, measures not applied since the cases of Edward Schillebeeckx and Hans Küng. They gave me their solemn assurance that my case was no parallel. Nothing more was involved here than an "explanatory conversation" with His Eminence, they said. They stated their intention to fetch me by limousine on Friday. I protested, saying I would simply be driven to the offices of the Sacred Congregation by Father General and other confreres. But they insisted, and I referred them to Father General for a reply. Cardinal Ratzinger did contact Father General, on Friday itself, asking that he be allowed to have his secretary, Father Klemens, come to fetch me.

Dom Ivo Lorscheiter, President of the Brazilian Bishops' Conference, and Cardinal Aloísio Lorscheider had been in Rome for several days, paying visits to various Roman offices. They were also received in audience by the Holy Father, with whom they discussed my case, and who averred that he had read, with gratification, a number of works of mine, but not *Igreja: carisma e poder*, presently under adjudication. Our prelates also visited Cardinal Ratzinger, seeking permission to be present at the "conversation." But, as such participation was not provided for in the *Ratio Agendi*, and lest a precedent be set, their petition was denied. Cardinal Aloísio cited the fact of his presidency of the Brazilian Bishops' Doctrinal Commission as justification for at least his mute presence at the conversation. Cardinal Ratzinger declined to render a decision on this new petition, forwarding it instead to the Secretary of State, Cardinal Casaroli.

From this conversation at the Sacred Congregation, I could see that my "conversation" would be an official *colloquium*, held according to the official rules of procedure of the Congregation. There was to be a stenographer, in the person of Argentinian Father Jorge Mejía. I would be permitted to take the minutes of the meeting to my quarters, study them, recommend modifications, and sign them. Finally, the "conversation" was not to be a simple conversation after all, as Cardinal Ratzinger's emissaries had promised it would be. So I spent an entire day studying Father Schillebeeckx' *colloquium,* which had been published in the periodical *Il Regno* in 1979 and 1980.

On September 6, Cardinal Arns of São Paulo joined the other prelates in Rome and earnestly sought to be allowed to assist at the colloquium, since he wished to offer his support to a former student, a friend, and a fellow Franciscan, as well as to testify to the ecclesial nature of the reflection being carried on in Brazil, since this reflection was conducted in strict communication with and dependence on the bishops and in strict respect for the pastoral orientation of the Church.

Our prelates obtained an audience with Secretary of State Cardinal Casaroli, who showed himself to be very receptive to their request to be allowed to assist at the colloquium. In spite of some reluctance, he acceded, thereby altering the nature of the meeting. Now it would no longer be subject to the formal rules of the Sacred Congregation, but indeed a simple explanatory conversation. And now our cardinals could be present.

The meeting would be divided into two sessions. In the first, I would be conversing with Cardinal Ratzinger. In the second, the Brazilian cardinals would join us.

The press had reported, not always without a touch of sensationalism, Cardinal Ratzinger's assertion that I had come to Rome of my own initiative to solicit the opinion of the Sacred Congregation with respect to the debate raging in Brazil. Through Cardinal Lorscheider I sought to point out to the Prefect of the Congregation, Cardinal Ratzinger, the baselessness of this assertion and asked for a retraction, seeing how much confusion his statement had caused in the media. Cardinal Ratzinger then directed the Printing Office, under Father Panciroli, to draw up a retraction, in curial style, entitled, "Precisions upon the Colloquium with Father Boff." There the basic data were finally given— including my summons to Rome "for September 7"! The meeting would not be on the eighth after all, then, as the Apostolic Nuncio to Brazil had informed me it would be.

On Friday morning, September 7, I celebrated Mass with the cardinals, my brother Clodovis, my sister Lina, and another brother of ours who taught in Brussels, in the chapel of the Franciscan headquarters. The atmosphere was charged with a sense of communion. Our people were celebrating their independence today—an independence not yet complete. We celebrated our communion with the Church and with the Apostolic See. We celebrated our communion with the Sacred Congregation for the Doctrine of the Faith, whose task it was zealously to guard and foster the truth of our faith. It was not a matter of who would be the winners and losers. What counted was how we might all demonstrate the power of the Gospel, lived in Church, as the integral promotion and liberation of all the oppressed.

At 9:40 A.M., personnel of the Sacred Congregation called for me. Once more I sought permission to be accompanied as far as the door of the Sacred Congregation by my Superior General. Again I was refused. Once more I screwed up my courage and asked that some of my fellow Franciscans be permitted to accompany me in the limousine. But once more Cardinal Ratzinger's secretary insisted we abide by what had been decided.

I attempted to lighten the tense atmosphere with a little humor. "Too bad I'm not just plain under arrest!" I quipped. "Then this could go down as a 'first' in the *modern* history of the Congregation!" I made another attempt some minutes later, when, after a very high-speed trip through the narrow Roman streets, we arrived at the huge iron grill of the portico of the Congregation's offices. I asked my two tense—and humiliated and embarrassed—companions, "Ah, the torture chamber?" This time we all "unbent" and relaxed, laughed, and jostled one another amicably.

Cardinal Ratzinger received me all smiles. I greeted him in German and was immediately led to the conference table. Once more I requested a correction of the statement in the papers to the effect that I was in Rome on my own initiative rather than at the express request of the Prefect of the Congregation. Cardinal Ratzinger repeated that the journalists had simply "misunderstood." I remarked that the *Osservatore Romano,* the official organ of the Holy See, had said the same thing, on September 4. But His Eminence merely smiled and motioned to me to be seated. I asked him to pray with me to the Holy Spirit, as this was the usage among Christians. His Eminence took a prayer book from the table, and we prayed the *Veni, Sancte Spiritus* together—"Come, Holy Spirit."

The Cardinal Prefect opened the conversation by offering me ample opportunity to say anything I wished. I might even read the whole of my prepared text. I read a long introduction on the historico-social reality of Brazil, the position of the Church in the situation, and the matter of theological reflection on the Church and on society. I then selected a number of points in the six-page letter that His Eminence had addressed to me and responded to them from my prepared text. The Cardinal followed my remarks with the utmost attention and interest.

At one point a bit of discussion arose, on the relationship among the "Church of Christ," the "Roman Catholic Church," and the "other Christian Churches." The Second Vatican Council, I pointed out, had been the scene of an internal evolution on this question. At first it had been proposed purely and simply to identify the Church of Christ with the Roman Catholic Church: "Ecclesia Christi *est* Ecclesia catholica. . . ." But then discussions on the presence of ecclesial elements in the other Christian communities and Churches had arisen, occasioning the removal of the "est" and the substitution of "subsistit in"— with the result that in the text of *Lumen Gentium*, no. 8, as we have it today, we read: "The Church of Christ *subsists in* [instead of 'is'] the Catholic Church." The oneness between the Church of Christ and the Catholic Church, then, is dynamic and not static, I argued. The Church of Christ is *realized*, is concretely actualized, in the Catholic Church as the essentially, constitutively dynamic reality of being the "sacramental of the Church." I do not say, I pointed out, that the Church of Christ nowhere subsists. It subsists in the Roman Catholic Church. But it subsists there in the concrete form of shadow and fidelity (*Lumen Gentium*, no. 8). After all, "many elements and positive values, and excellent ones, with which the Church as a whole is constructed and vivified can exist outside the pale of the Catholic Church" (*Unitatis Redintegratio*, no. 3). Cardinal Ratzinger disagreed with my interpretation of the passage from the Vatican II document, holding that "subsistit" has the sense of substance, and that, as substance can be only one, the Church of Christ must therefore subsist in the Catholic Church alone. He reminded me that he had been a member of the theological commission that had drawn up the document, and insisted that this is what the Commission had actually meant by the expression in question. After our meeting I studied all the texts and theologians' reports bearing on the theme in the *Acta Synodalia,* or minutes of the commissions and committees. In no instance did "subsistit in" have the sense of substance. In every case it meant "concretely to be found, to be present, to exist in." Nor does Forcellini's huge *Totius Latinitatis Lexicon,* I saw, while distinguishing twelve meanings of *subsistere,* admit of one corresponding to *substantia.* All twelve meanings denote *subsistentia,* or concrete reality. Thus even "the dictionary" confirmed my version of the meaning intended by the theological commission for the Council's declaration, "Ecclesia Christi subsistit in Ecclesia catholica." Cardinal Aloísio Lorscheider, who had been a member of the Commission along with Cardinal Ratzinger, was of the same mind as I.

But to return to the day of the meeting itself: After two hours of conversation between Cardinal Ratzinger and myself, Cardinals Aloísio Lorscheider and Paulo Evaristo Arns entered the room, along with the Secretary of the Sacred Congregation for the doctrine of the Faith, Bishop Alberto Bovone, and the discussion continued. The most important intervention was on the part of Cardinal Arns, who suggested to the Congregation that the promised new document, on the positive wealth to be found in the theology of liberation, should, first of all, be prepared in consultation with the "engineers" of that theology, the theologians who for years have been constructing this theological current; second, that it should be prepared in consultation with the episcopate, as it is they who perform the pastoral activity among the people, walking with the oppressed along the highways and byways of liberation, so that the ecclesial and pastoral dimensions of this new theological current could enjoy adequate emphasis in the new document; and third, that the document should be actually prepared in the Third World, in Africa or Latin America, for instance, amidst the actual reality of the poverty and oppression in which the theology of liberation has its point of departure, since this would tend to bring the text of the new document straight to the heart of things, and do justice to the cause of the oppressed. Cardinal Ratzinger timidly agreed with all three of Cardinal Arns' points.

Finally, a joint communiqué was carefully drawn up:

On September 7, 1984, at 10:00 A.M., in the offices of the Sacred Congregation for the Doctrine of the Faith, the Reverend Father Leonardo Boff, O.F.M., was received by His Eminence, Cardinal Joseph Ratzinger, Prefect of the same Congregation, for purposes of a conversation. The Cardinal Prefect was assisted by Monsignor Joseph Mejía. The subject of their conversation was the letter written by the Cardinal Prefect to the Reverend Father Leonardo Boff, under date of the fifteenth of May of this year, on certain problems arising from a reading of his book, *Igreja: carisma e poder.* The intent of the conversation was to afford Father Boff, in view of the previously determined publication of the said letter, an opportunity to explain certain aspects of the book that were cited in the letter and that had created difficulty. The Sacred Congregation will take under advisement, via its customary protocol, suitable ways of making public, along with the publication of the letter itself, any germane results of the conversation. The conversation was carried on in the spirit of brotherhood. The present communiqué is a joint one.

The major significance of the presence of the two Brazilian cardinals was, surely, that of testifying to the ecclesial character of the theology being developed in Brazil. That theology may contain ambiguities. It may even contain errors. But it strives to be a theology within the Church and to the benefit of the Church. Ambiguities can be explained and errors corrected: neither deprive theology of its legitimate place in the pilgrim journey of our Church. This point was amply established. A happy precedent may have been created for the handling of similar situations by the Sacred Congregation for the Doctrine of the Faith.

The conversation was followed by a week of interviews with the various media. The affair had stirred a great deal of interest in many parts of the world. I was interviewed by Korean, Japanese, Finnish, Norwegian, German, United States, British, Brazilian, and so on, television networks, each representing a number of affiliates in its respective country. Once the official conversation had been held a great number of others followed, both in Brazil and abroad. I consented to numerous interviews on condition that they would not be restricted to my own personal issue but would deal with liberation, justice, and the Christian responsibility for transformations inspired by the Gospel and the great tradition of the Church.

Lessons to Be Learned

A summons by the highest doctrinal office of the Roman Catholic Church is no commonplace event in the life of a theologian—still less in that of a theologian of the "periphery," whose theology is produced in conditions so unlike those of the great metropolitan centers of reflection. It is surely memorable—in fact, shattering—suddenly to find oneself in the public gaze and incarnating, for a goodly number of people, for a brief moment, the substance and destiny of a whole current of thought and of ecclesial experience. The sense and meaning of a like event escapes subjective evaluation. And in the present instance, procedures are not always easy to grasp. I learned from a member of the Congregation itself that in May a Brazilian prelate, whose full name my informant was unable to recall but who once had been connected with Caritas Catholica, had been in Rome seeking the condemnation of my *Igreja: carisma e poder,* and seeking it so persistently that he became an annoyance. From another Vatican source I learned that the Holy Father himself, who in matters of doctrine of course always has the final word, upon reading the May 15 letter written to me by Cardinal Ratzinger, with its criticisms and even condemnation of my book, asked whether these matters had ever been discussed personally with Father Boff. On hearing that they had not, he forbade publication of the letter and requested that I be summoned for a *colloquium*. Had it not been for the Holy Father's personal intervention, then, the letter would have been published without previous consultation, written or oral, with me.

As I have said above there are lessons to be learned from this story. In the first place, I could feel a mighty current of solidarity with thousands of my fellow Christians the length and breadth of our land—from the bishops to the simple members of the base communities—as well as in many other parts of the world, from Poland to New Zealand. These expressions of solidarity were less for me than for the cause of the value of a local church and the status of the theology it develops. It is totally baseless, indeed it is insulting, to understand this solidarity—of the highest ecclesial value as an expression of communion—as a disparagement of the office and person of the Holy Father or of the Apostolic See.

Second, the event and the discussion that was held meant that a genuine process of evangelization was under way, not so much via ecclesiastical channels, but via the secular channels of the media. The latter understood perfectly well what the real question was: commitment to the poor, to the profound societal changes that are so necessary, and to the liberation of the oppressed. This is a question transcending the frontiers of the churches. It is of concern to all; it affects conscience. Thus it signifies a universal political challenge. For over twenty years, our churches and their liberation theology have been reflecting in the midst of this drama, with their own resources of faith, the discipleship of Jesus, and the modern application of the Gospel. And they have been sketching out pertinent Christian responses to this universal challenge. A great many people now see more clearly than ever before what it means to do theology today: It means to "think God" as the One who maintains an intimate involvement with the human journey in search of higher and more excellent forms of fellowship and communion in justice, peace, and participation. And it means "thinking the human pilgrimage," marked by such iniquity, along with such generosity, in the light of God and his historical revelation in the Old and New Testaments, a revelation preserved in the historical Christian community of today. Theology can represent one of the most estimable forms—the most excellent, surely—of the identification of human destiny in history and in the realm of the transcendent.

Finally, the whole affair evinces once again the limitation and finitude of all things created, including the organs of Church authority, necessary as these are for the proclamation and promotion of the Christian faith. As the wise and saintly Father Yves M.-J. Congar wrote in *La Croix* on September 9, 1984, just at the time of my Roman ordeal, on the subject of the "charism of central power," this power is the power of not having doubts about oneself. And he went on:

Now, not to have doubts about oneself is a thing at once magnificent and terrible—magnificent, because the charism of the center consists precisely in standing firm when everything about quakes and trembles; and terrible, because human beings in Rome have their limits, their limits in intelligence, in vocabulary, in background, in viewpoint.

Despite these limits, surely we ought not to view these human beings as performing their task in the spirit of the Grand Inquisitor, but rather in that of brothers in faith with ourselves, persons seeking to discharge their arduous task and mission of zealously preserving the basic tenets of our faith and the mainstays of our hope. This task is done sometimes correctly and properly, sometimes incorrectly and improperly, but always with the intention of being faithful to that Word that ultimately will judge us all.

I went to Rome as a Catholic theologian. I returned from Rome as a Catholic theologian. I hope to be able to continue with my ministry of reflection, within the pilgrim process of our Church, in a communion open in every direction, learning as I go, and giving of the little I shall have learned, with humility and courage, as a servant of the Gospel who has only done what was expected of him (see Luke 17:10).

Leonardo Boff, o.f.m.
Frater, theologus minor et peccator

16

THE VALUE OF RESISTANCE

Disciplinary measures taken against Friar Leonardo Boff prevent his speaking openly or publishing for at least a year. Accordingly, he may not recount to the world what has occurred in his regard since his summons to Rome and his meeting with the Cardinal Prefect of the Congregation for the Doctrine of the Faith on September 7, 1984. I shall take the liberty of speaking for my brother, then, and recount the events of the eleven-month period in question, succinctly, and with an eye only to the public, objective aspect of the case.

Leonardo Boff's summons to Rome stirred enormous public interest in the theology of liberation. Of a sudden this theology seemed to "hit the streets." One could hear it discussed even in cafes, the market place, everywhere.

In response to this interest Leonardo spent a great deal of time after his return to Brazil, in mid-September, 1984, presenting and discussing liberation theology in response to invitations by popular groups, universities, labor unions, and various radio and television stations. Invitations arrived from all over the world. It seemed as if everyone in the universities suddenly wanted a talk or a course by Boff: in North America, Europe, and Latin America. Faithful to his theological opinion, however, Leonardo chose to remain in Brazil, and there strive to consolidate a theological reflection undertaken in solidarity with the Christian communities.

One wonders whether liberation theology would have made the "waves" it has today had it not been for the wide debate provoked by the Ratzinger-Boff dialogue, along with the publication by the Congregation for the Doctrine of the Faith of the "Instruction on Certain Aspects of the 'Theology of Liberation.'" Both events occured in the same week, in Rome. The *Instruction* was officially promulgated on September 4, and Leonardo met with Cardinal Ratzinger three days later. There are indications that this near-simultaneity was intentional on the part of the Congregation, as Rome had refused Leonardo's request to hold the meeting in early October—scheduling it for "September 7 or 8," instead.

As previously noted, on March 19, 1984, a representative of Apostolic Nuncio to Brazil Archbishop Carlo Furno formally handed Friar Leonardo Boff, in Petrópolis, Brazil, where Leonardo lives and works, a "Notification Concerning the Book, *Igreja: carisma e poder.*" The document—eleven pages printed by Tipografia Poliglotta Vaticana—consisted of an analysis of positions it attributed to Leonardo concerning the structure of the Church, dogma and revelation, the exercise of Church authority, and the propheticism of the Church. In conclusion, the document, approved by Pope John Paul II under date of March 11, 1985, stated: "The Congregation feels itself under obligation to declare the options of Friar Leonardo Boff, here analyzed, to be of such a nature as to imperil the sound doctrine of the Church, which this same Congregation has the duty of fostering and safeguarding."

In a press release March 20, Leonardo repeated what he had said earlier: "I had rather journey with the Church than walk with my own theology and walk alone." But Leonardo also called attention to the fact that the Roman document had not appeared in the form of a *monitum*, an "admonition," but bore the simple appellation of "notification." It did not, then, involve any sort of condemnation. It was simply a notification of certain reservations regarding what Leonardo seemed to the Congregation to be teaching, without qualifying any of it as "heretical, schismatical, or impious." It labeled these supposed teachings with the qualification corresponding to the lowest degree of dogmatic censure: "dangerous to the sound teaching of the faith."

Leonardo accepted the Holy See's intervention in the spirit of religious loyalty and obedience. In a letter to His Holiness Pope John Paul II, dated March 30, 1984, the author of *Igreja: carisma e poder* reiterated his respect for the highest doctrinal organ of the Church, the Congregation for the Doctrine of the Faith, but acknowledged, "with a certain sorrow, that the 'Notification' of the Congregation for the Doctrine of the Faith could have referred to my positions on pages 71, 109, 128, 131, and 248–49 [of the book in question] with more accuracy."

Indeed, the Freckenhorster Kreis, a group of some two hundred laity, priests, and theologians of the Diocese of Münster, Germany, issued a minutely detailed study of the "Notification," calling attention to its erroneous quotations and other misrepresentations. "With methods like this," it concluded, "it would not be difficult to denounce passages from Ratzinger, the popes, and Scripture itself" ("Die Lesehilfe des Freckenhorster Kreis," in *Publick-Forum Sonderdruck*, p. v).

Under date of April 26, 1985, Cardinals Joseph Ratzinger, of the Congregation for the Doctrine of the Faith, and Jerome Hamer, Prefect of the Congregation of Religious and of Secular Institutes, dispatched a letter to Father General John Vaughn of the Franciscans, imposing three disciplinary measures on Leonardo: (1) "a period of silence under obedience," unspecified in length, but "of sufficient duration to afford him a space for adequate reflection," and also suspending his various activities as speaker, retreat director, and consultant at conventions and meetings; (2) the renunciation of his responsibilities on the editorial staff of *Revista Eclesiástica Brasileira,* the "Brazilian Ecclesiastical Review" that Leonardo had edited for many years; and (3) submission to previous censorship, to be applied with "particular care, including conformity with the prevailing norms of the Church and if need be of the Constitutions of the [Franciscan] Order that this means may have its effect," of any theological writing that Leonardo might do. In a letter to Leonardo dated May 2, 1985, Father General Vaughn, as Leonardo's religious superior charged with the implementation of the disciplinary measures taken against him by the two Roman congregations, while expressing profound solidarity with his Brazilian confrere, and being under constraint, asked Leonardo to abide by the decisions of the Holy See, and specified the period of "silence under obedience" as to be of one year's duration. Exempt from the ban, Father Vaughn further specified, would be homilies at the Eucharist and lectures in theology to Franciscan seminarians in Petrópolis, these latter not being open to the public.

The measures provoked loud public outcry, in Brazil as throughout the world. Leonardo accepted the decision, and before entering his period of penitential silence made the following declaration.

I declare that I am not a Marxist. As a Christian and Franciscan I favor liberties, the rights of religion, and the noble struggle for justice and toward a new society. I reaffirm that the Gospel is addressed to all human beings without exception, while at the same time recognizing that this same Gospel gives priority to the poor, as it is they who constitute the suffering majorities, so that it is they who are the favorites of God, of Christ, and of the Church. It is my view that, in a situation of oppression such as ours, the mission of the Church ought to be unambiguously liberative. I am convinced that the measures taken in my regard in no way abolish the need to proceed in the development of an authentic theology of liberation, in communion with the magisterium of the Church.

From this moment forward it will be incumbent upon the competent authorities to furnish any further information.

The measures taken by the two Roman cardinals caused a great deal of scandal in Brazil, in view of the political context of the early months of 1985, when the country was emerging from a military dictatorship characterized by all manner of arbitrary procedures, the abolition of the right of free speech, and the most severe censorship. The Church had performed its prophetic role, criticizing this state of affairs and helping to create a spirit of democracy. Then, at the very moment that the Church had at last won back its liberties, it had to witness the painful spectacle of Rome's utilization of the very methods used by the military and criticized by the Brazilian bishops. Ten bishops, with an archbishop at their head who had been considered the patriarch of the struggle against the military dictatorship, Dom Fernando Gomes dos Santos, of Goiâna, some 130 kilometers from Brasilia, publicly criticized Rome and defended Leonardo. Thousands of letters and signatures arrived from all over the world in support of the Franciscan theologian, especially from the base communities of Brazil.

Two eminent attorneys, Dr. Helio Bicudo and Dr. José Queiroz, of São Paulo, celebrated for their defense of political prisoners and their campaign against the death squads, in the name of hundreds of centers for the defense of human rights, and of Justice and Peace action groups, mounted a juridical appeal to the Holy See for the rescission of the punitive measures taken against Leonardo. Subsequently they took the same action in the courts of Geneva and The Hague. With great difficulty they finally succeeded in having their petition filed with the President of the Pontifical Commission for Justice and Peace.

On June 11, 1985, the President of the National Conference of Brazilian Bishops, Dom Ivo Lorscheiter, held a long conversation with the Holy Father in Rome concerning the perplexities being occasioned in Brazil, in Church and civil society alike, by the behavior of the Congregation for the Doctrine of the Faith. It had taken its disciplinary measures without any previous contact with the Brazilian Bishops' Conference or with the Bishops' Commission on Doctrine, thus undermining the meaning of collegiality and ultimately doing a disservice to evangelization. He handed the Pope a thick dossier of newspaper reports, along with copies of letters received by the Bishops' Conference, expressing astonishment that such usages should still prevail in Rome. He conceded the right, and under certain conditions the duty, of the Holy See to intervene in these matters. This was beyond all question. In question was only the authoritarian manner in which this intervention was occurring. The popular consciousness had by now been raised to a level that no longer tolerated disciplinary tools like these. The people expected such procedures to have been relegated to utilization by Latin American military regimes.

The upshot of Dom Ivo's audience with the Holy Father was the decision to arrange a meeting between the Brazilian Bishops' Conference Steering Committee—consisting of their Excellencies, Ivo Lorscheiter, Luciano Mendes de Almeida, and Benedito Ulhoa Vieira—the Bishops' Commission for Doctrine—consisting of Cardinal Aloísio Lorscheider as President and four other bishops—with the Roman Congregation for the Doctrine of the Faith. The agenda would include future procedures, as well as the significance of theology in a local Church that, by reason of its pastoral liberation practice, stands in need of serious theological reflection.

The meeting was held on July 4 and 5, in Rome—eight hours, in all, of debate and a sharing of experience, in which the "reference manuals" were the documents of Vatican II and the new Code of Canon Law. Some of the conclusions emerging from these conversations were later published in the *Boletim Semanal* ("Weekly Bulletin") of the Brazilian Bishops' Conference (July 25, 1985, no. 790). The "Boff case" implied no new judgment rendered on the theology of liberation; by the end of 1985 a new document would be published, in which the positive aspects of that theology would be emphasized; the document would have the benefit of previous consultation with the national Bishops' Conferences (as Cardinal Arns, it will be recalled, had explicitly requested); the restrictions on Boff did not mean absolute silence, since, as we have seen, he was still permitted to preach at Mass and lecture in theology to the Petrópolis Friars; the Vatican would take increased account of the principle of subsidiarity in its relations with the Brazilian Bishops' Conference, and problems would "go to Rome" only after the Church of Brazil had exhausted its internal resources; the Brazilian Bishops' Doctrinal Commission would continue to function in a positive, and not inquisitorial manner.

On July 29, 1985, the Vatican Secretary of State, Cardinal

Casaroli, acting in the name and at the behest of His Holiness Pope John Paul II, wrote a letter to Leonardo in which he sought to construe the measures taken by the Holy See in a positive manner, in an evident effort to deprive them of their punitive character. The letter read, in part:

The measures taken constitute no impediment to continued theological work on the part of Your Reverence. . . . What is actually required is the observance of certain restrictions, among which the "silence of obedience" is intended to afford you an interim for the rethinking, before God, of problems of such great import for a theologian, as well as to reflect on your responsibilities to your brothers in the faith.

It may be hoped that, as of this date, and in view of the Extraordinary Synod, held in Rome, and in view of Leonardo's scrupulous observance of the measures taken by the Congregation, along with the intercession of the National Conference of Brazilian Bishops, who came out so strongly in support of their theologian, the term of the "silence of obedience" may be abbreviated, or even that all the disciplinary measures may be suspended.

It would be premature to attempt to make a conclusive assessment of the Boff Case and its repercussions on Church and society. One thing, however, is altogether clear: that it has served as a powerful factor for conscientization, for consciousness-raising, in the sense of an ever more deeply felt need to get beyond authoritarian forms of relationship within the Church to an awareness of the importance of "human rights for Christians too," and a new courage on the part of the National Conferences to defend the legitimacy of a theological thought accompanying a pastoral practice as a right of the local Church itself.

Finally, the behavior of the Roman authorities has served fully to justify the criticisms leveled in *Igreja: carisma e poder* against the mechanisms maintained by the central authorities of the Church.

What remains open is the challenge to conversion, not only of persons in the Church, but of the structures through which power in the Church is distributed and exercised.

Clodovis Boff
August 20, 1985